'Best Year Yet made a huge differenc... dition. It is a truly wonderful, powerful and effective tool.'

Erik Weihenmayer, first blind climber to reach the top of Mount Everest

'Jinny came into my life when I needed her most. She listened, helped, cajoled and inspired. She is a friend, guide and teacher. I often wished that everyone could have the opportunity to grow with her. This book will hopefully be a first step for many. I am a fan.'

Bill Kenwright, Producer, London

'My work with Jinny enabled me to resolve the paradox between having the life I wanted for myself and worrying that I didn't deserve it.'

Martin Shaw, Actor

'Best Year Yet has proven to be an excellent means of improving our business performance. It ensured the successful launch of Dalcassian Wines & Spirits and is supporting the ongoing business development – the monthly reviews are really keeping us on track. The whole team supports the process – it has been pivotal to our success.'

Pat Rigney, Managing Director, Dalcassian Wines & Spirits Ltd

'Most management teams fail to spend enough time on strategic planning, documenting short term goals and communication between senior executives. Best Year Yet provides an efficient and effective conduit which forces us to proactively address issues and track progress on a monthly basis. It is an excellent investment of managed capital.

Best Year Yet has improved communication and ensures that all members of the team are rowing in the same direction.'

Steve Keaveney, Managing Director, Broadworks Communications Ltd

'Best Year Yet is a highly successful programme, challenging us to take a hard look at the business and ourselves and leading to a sharp focus on our personal and corporate goals.'

Roland Alden, Managing Director, Bank of Ireland (IOM)

'The personal Best Year Yet programme is the most effective personal organization tool I have ever used. The team programme has produced great results for my top team.'

Chris Gillies, Managing Director, Zurich Intermediary Group, Zurich Financial Services

'I'd recommend Best Year Yet for any leader looking for a sense of direction and ownership amongst their team, while creating an ability to influence the wider business.'

Paul Stanley, Head of Regulated Sales, Halifax, plc

'We are halfway through our first year and the Best Year Yet Team programme has already had a significant impact on our team and its vision. The structure of the programme brought the team together as never before, encouraged sharing of concerns, opened our minds and allowed us to think the previously unthinkable. It is easy to be cynical about packaged management courses, but this is an excellent vehicle and particularly well delivered by Ralph Peters who is outstanding at adapting it to the client's needs.'

John Sweeting, Chief Executive, Treloar Trust

'We needed something to make senior managers accountable for building the *entire* bank. Best Year Yet is the solution!'

Scott Bradley, President, Pinnacle Bank, USA

'Best Year Yet is not complicated. All the programme asks of you is to do it and keep doing it! The results from my team speak for themselves – we moved from last place in the country to first in the highly challenging environment of sales and service. Best Year Yet played a big part and will do again as I take on a new and much bigger team this year.'

David McAvoy, Regional Managing Director, NatWest Retail Bank

'Best Year Yet is a focused system that changes behaviour, culture and performance, time after time.'

Lawrence Churchill, former CEO, Zurich Financial Services, UK

'Best Year Yet represents a breakthrough in coaching and consulting. I think it's a wonderful programme for professionals to use with their clients.'

Robert Middleton, President, Action Plan Marketing International

'The results were tremendous. I have achieved organization, focus and comfort in my business and life. After attending the seminar and putting into motion the things I learned, I truly did have my best year yet.

I would recommend the Best Year Yet to anyone who wishes to make change, needs a boost or simply would like to refocus what is happening in their life.'

Dennis Farn, Estate Agent, Remax Real Estate

'One of the biggest accomplishments for me was to write a book, and I have already completed my second draft and I believe I have a publisher for it. Another biggie was my trip to Ireland with my husband. We have tried to find time to go for years and I am happy to announce I just got back from my dream trip to the Emerald Isle.

I can honestly say that I accomplished those goals because of those few hours I took out of my schedule to organize and get real with my life with the Best Year Yet programme.'

Vickie Kallman, speaker and author

'I found Best Year Yet to be a rare opportunity to integrate personal and business goals in a lively, energizing format '

Sandy Gorby Welches, Human Resources Manager

YOUR
BEST
YEAR
YET

JINNY DITZLER

HARPER
element

HarperElement
An Imprint of HarperCollins*Publishers*
77-85 Fulham Palace Road,
Hammersmith, London W6 8JB

The website address is: www.thorsonselement.com

element™ and *HarperElement* are trademarks of
HarperCollins*Publishers* Ltd

First published by Thorsons 1994
This edition published by HarperElement 2006

24

ISBN-13 978-0-00-722322-0
ISBN-10 0-00-722322-6

Printed and bound in Great Britain by
Clays Ltd, St Ives plc

To Tim,
With my love and deep appreciation.

But there is such a thing as genuine love, which is always considerate.
Its distinguishing characteristic is, in fact, regard for personal dignity.
Its effect is to stimulate self-respect in the other person. Its concern is to
help the loved one become their true self. In a mysterious way such love
finds its truest realization in its power to stimulate the other to attain
their highest self-realization.

ROMANO GUARDINI

CONTENTS

ACKNOWLEDGMENTS

One of the biggest blessings of writing this book is the opportunity to say a public 'thank you' to the people who have taught me and helped me so much. Without them, this book and the work I do would have been impossible:

to all the participants in all the Best Year Yet Workshops – you have proven it works and inspired me to pass it on

to each of my clients: you have trusted me and allowed me to share so fully in your life – in your presence I have learned the secrets I share here

to my friends Jock and Susie, who said 'DO IT!' loud enough for me to hear

to our Support group, who have been my British family for the past thirteen years

to my greatest teachers: Werner Erhard, who gave me the keys to my power; John-Roger, who opened my heart; and Lew Epstein, who showed me how to let myself be loved

to my courageous colleagues and partners in Results Unlimited and The Results Partnership, who carved the path for transformation in the UK in the tough years before there was a demand for it

to Celia Brayfield, who wrote about her work with me long before it was safe to do so

to Val Corbett, creator and producer of *Executive Coach*, who saw something in me I hadn't seen myself and then helped me to share it so powerfully

to my agent, Bruce Hyman, whose persistent commitment and intelligent insight have raised the level of this pursuit far beyond anything I could have done myself

to my editor, Jane Graham-Maw, who believed strongly in the project from the first moment and made it seem so easy

to my coach, Roger Cadman, who relentlessly supported me to practise what I preach

to my parents, Leo Eugene Anderson and Katherine Thomas Anderson, whose keen intelligence and strong will I have inherited but whose love has meant everything

to my wonderful big family who have encouraged me at every step, been proud of me and helped me believe in myself

to my sons, who have honoured me with their unconditional love – and who have made me so proud

and, most of all, to my husband Tim, who has given me the blessing of unconditional love and the joy of sleeping with my biggest fan!

WELCOME

I invite you to have your best year ever – year after year – for the rest of your life.

The Best Year Yet experience is designed to reach the core of how you think and perform, and to empower you to new levels of personal effectiveness and fulfilment. In a three-hour process of self-discovery, you stand back, take stock and then plan the next year of your life. The exercise of answering ten simple questions helps you to clarify your thinking and make sure your next year is the best it can be. At the end of your personal workshop you'll have a simple one-page plan to guide you through your next twelve months.

This format has been used by hundreds of people over the past fourteen years and together we have shaped and simplified the annual life review and planning process to a point of profound power. Yes, we've been able to improve our ability to make things happen, and many, many of us are more successful financially, in our careers and in our relationships. But more important, we're taking the time to gain an overview which gives us a better chance to give meaning to our lives and what we do. It brings us to a new level of consciousness and awareness in the way we live and direct our own lives.

Many, many people have carried out this exercise on an annual basis for years; it has helped them to create a fundamental shift in their lives and given them the satisfaction of achieving the results that really matter to them. As one friend says so eloquently,

> I saw that I wasn't living the way I wanted to be and now I've stopped
> postponing a lot of things that are dear to me.

So many have learned to take the lead in their own lives – it's a beautiful sight. I've used this same process for myself and I'm astounded at what I've achieved and how I've grown as a person. Every year since the first has somehow, in some way, been my best year yet. So, as I often say to participants in the workshop, *If a school teacher from Nebraska can do it, so can you!*

Again, I welcome and invite you to join us on your own journey of increasing self-respect that comes from living your life in a way that reflects what matters most to you.

HOW TO USE THIS BOOK

The public workshop is an all-day event, but over the years many people have been doing it on their own, usually taking about three hours to get through the ten questions. Watching them succeed so well on their own helped me to realize that this really is a simple do-it-yourself process.

Many people create their Best Year Yet plan in January so they can plan the calendar year ahead. But the process of reflection and planning can be done at any time of the year with equal success. Don't think of this as a book that's only about January to January – if you're reading it now, then now's the time to answer the questions, believe you can do it and get on with it.

This book is divided into three parts:

PART ONE: An introduction to the principles on which Best Year Yet is based, as well as a sharing of the experiences of many people who have participated in the process.

PART TWO: Each of the ten questions has its own chapter in which I review the background material and provide further explanation to help you to answer each question for yourself.

PART THREE: Your own Best Year Yet Workshop, with space for you to answer each of the questions and write your own one-page plan for the next twelve months.

You will of course have your own style for doing things; depending on what that is, pick your approach to Your Best Year Yet from these options:

1. Turn immediately to PART THREE and start answering the Ten Best Year Yet questions. If you want help or explanations as you go along, turn to the chapter in PART TWO which relates to the question you're working on.
2. Read PARTS ONE and TWO as preparation for your workshop, perhaps making notes as you read. When you've finished, set aside three hours and write your answers to the questions in PART THREE.

Whatever your choice, enjoy the journey!

THE TURNING POINT

The idea started on New Year's Day in 1980, when my boyfriend (now my husband) Tim and I woke up in our flat in London. We'd been working in Britain for less than a year and living together only a couple of months, having met shortly after we both arrived from different parts of the US the previous spring.

Perhaps I needed a bit of a distraction as I'd given up smoking the night before and had made such a public fuss there was no turning back. Or maybe it was the thought of the new decade ahead. Who knows? But for the first time for ages I began to think a bit more seriously about the year ahead. And before we even left our bed, I suggested that we run a marathon, and Tim agreed.

This was the only goal I remember setting that year, probably because we hadn't decided to stay together and thinking ahead was a tentative business – we weren't really at the point of planning a life together.

We picked the Paris Marathon, scheduled for May. The goal may not seem unusual today, but 1980 was a year before the birth of the London Marathon and the sight of a runner on the road – particularly a woman – was still cause for staring and pointing.

We started to train and, although we'd been in the habit of jogging a couple of miles several days a week, we were told we needed a new regime, working our way up to over 50 miles a week in the last month before the marathon. Gradually we began to lengthen our pre-work circuit of Bishops Park in Fulham to runs over Putney Bridge, up the towpath, under the Hammersmith Bridge and on until we reached whatever point was halfway to our target time for the day, then turning back towards home along the same route we'd come.

By mid-March we began to see the end of the winter mornings and were starting to feel better about it all. As we talked with friends, some of them became interested and soon what began as a ridiculous conversation on the first day in January started to have a life of its own. In the end nearly a hundred of us went to Paris in two coaches, had a great time and raised thousands of pounds for charity.

But it was painful beyond belief – I thought it would never end and for Tim it was even worse. We ran the entire marathon side by side. At one point he was in such agony and so delirious that after a water stop at Mile 20 he started running back towards the starting line! But we did it. And the feeling of confidence and elation at having set and achieved such an outrageous goal lived long past the finish line. I learned, above all, how to keep going regardless, and in doing so found new strength and an ability I hadn't even known I had. I would never have discovered this if I hadn't forced myself to do so by going for this goal.

By the following New Year's Day in 1981 we were engaged to be married, still in the same rented flat and starting to think about planning the year ahead. We'd had a good year. The marathon was definitely a big thrill, but little else had really changed. Late in 1980 we decided to try to buy a place of our own, and in the process discovered that between us we had a *negative* net worth. It hadn't proved easy for either of us to build a career in London, and although we weren't too depressed about it all, the path ahead was not clear.

I had left a good job when it came time to transfer back to the US because I wanted to stay with Tim, but I hadn't yet found another job. We'd also had many long conversations about whether he really wanted to stay in the business world. We were happy together and having a good time but we were broke most of the time, allowing ourselves one monthly treat of dinner out at a local restaurant. But looking back it's easy to see that this day was a turning point for us.

It was on this day that the Best Year Yet workshop was really born, although I didn't start to lead the Best Year Yet courses for others until the following year. As we sat down to plan the coming year, common sense guided us to create this process. Before we started to think of the year ahead, it seemed natural to review 1980 and what had happened for each of us. Expecting the worst, we both found that we'd accomplished far more than we thought. We started to feel a bit more enthusiastic about ourselves and what lay ahead – an experience which, by the way, has proved to be the case for nearly everyone who has participated in the Best Year Yet programme over the years.

By the end of the day we had each set ourselves over a hundred goals. 1981 was definitely the best year yet for both of us – we were married, ran three more marathons, and each of us started our own business, both of which are still going today.

Still we ended the year with a low score because the sheer number of goals we had set made achieving all of them impossible.

When it came time to pass the idea on to others, it was obvious that having too many goals made it impossible to keep track of even half of them! The exercise has now been simplified to help us find our Top Ten Goals, and the whole process takes three hours or less.

But that first morning at the beginning of 1980 and our goal of running a marathon was the start of a new way of living for us. And once I turned the process into a workshop, more people had the chance to do the same for themselves; together we all found out a great deal about how to use our brains and our common sense to learn from the past year and make the best of the year ahead.

Tim and I have used the annual exercise in good times and in bad, taking time out every year to make sure we did it, no matter what. Just going through the process of coming up with our Top Ten Goals for the next year creates a powerful focus, even though there were some years when I would go for months before looking at the goals again. No two years are the same, obviously. Some years the focus of the goals is on money, some years fitness and well-being, some years relationships with family, some years working with my favourite charity and some years just facing up to challenges I couldn't possibly have predicted the year before.

We certainly haven't achieved all the goals we've set, and have hardly tracked our progress with robotic precision the way we always felt we should. But Best Year Yet has continued to provide a framework for our lives, building year on year, making sure we have at least the chance to learn the lessons of our past year and move on to our next goals. Sometimes when we come to the review at the end of the year we feel like the Torville and Dean of personal planning; other years it takes quite a bit of courage to look back. But we've kept at it for years now and it's made all the difference. There's no similarity between my life today and my life then, either in terms of the material accomplishments or in the quality of my life. I'm blessed with a lifestyle that's beyond anything I imagined as a child.

It's the discipline of Best Year Yet year after year that keeps us going and helps us continue to grow and learn. Things have not always been as good as they could have been, but when that happens I've learned to do my best to apply myself in the ways I've described in this book. Over the years, with the help of so many, Best Year Yet has evolved into a simple ten-question process that can be used by anyone, any time. While I hope I've learned by now that I have no right to impose my beliefs on anyone, I'm enthusiastic about passing this along because of what it's meant for me and so many others.

The best part for me has been my sense of self, the confidence I have, my appreciation for my particular talents, the way I'm able to work through life's knotty problems and the deep feeling that I'm doing a bit better all the time of living a life that's consistent with what I believe – these are the most important things that have come from the exercise of annual evaluation and planning.

Turning around to face life's most painful challenges has given me a growing personal strength and a deeper sense of who I am. And every time I'm able to do that myself, my ability to coach and encourage others to do the same is increased. *If I can do it, you can do it.* The effectiveness of my work with people keeps increasing as I get better and better at practising what I preach. But I'm still learning and always will be. I once heard a radio interview with Luciano Pavarotti in which he said he's never stopped taking singing lessons and doesn't intend to stop learning until the day he dies.

Inspired by Best Year Yet, Tim and I have come to do a little miniversion every week. We both work long hours and often don't see one another much during the week; several years ago this was eroding deeply into the quality of our marriage. The way we confronted that challenge, eventually not only restoring our love but deepening it, is one of the best examples of the transformation we've achieved.

About a year ago we starting having what we call our 'Friday night party', just the two of us. We get a bottle of wine, put on some music and sit and talk with each other until we catch up.

To balance the effect of some painful times, we started taking turns making toasts to the best things that had happened over the past week. Even in the worst weeks, there are those little miracles and things to be grateful for. It makes such a difference to remember to focus on how lucky we are rather than on what a struggle it all is.

And this is the real gift. If somehow we lost everything, we'd be strong enough to withstand it and start again or let it all go and live in a tent. I honestly believe that the inner strength we've developed can't be taken away and that we'll be all right regardless.

Above all, my motivation in writing this book is to make this kind of true success possible for you – to help you design a more meaningful life for yourself by giving you the means to becoming the master of your own destiny.

I've seen so many people who have made changes in their lives by taking the time to think about what they really want and then start taking steps to make it happen. Watching them over the years has inspired me to write about Best Year Yet and make it available to more people. You're never too old nor too young to make next year your best ever.

PART ONE

THREE HOURS TO CHANGE YOUR LIFE

INTRODUCTION

GOAL SETTING

Successful businesses set goals and plan ahead. They know that in order to generate the kind of important change and growth they're looking for, they must identify their priorities each year and then focus the energies of their people in such a way that these goals are achieved.

The secret of realizing this kind of success for ourselves is the same – setting goals and planning our lives a year at a time. In this way we too can deal with the bigger issues, address the concerns that really matter to us and make the kind of important changes we really want to make.

You know about goals – we all do. We've set them and even been successful in achieving many of them. By the age of eight or ten we begin to get an idea of what we want in life. A picture begins to form in our minds of a degree, a job, a car, a house, a family... and as we move through our teenage years our goals become even more clear to us. Soon we're 25 or 30 or 35 and we've achieved many of these early goals and trust we're on the way to the others. And new goals are already forming in our minds.

However, as life goes on, goal-setting becomes a more casual and far less specific process – wants and desires seem to arrive and plant themselves in our minds almost before we realize it. We don't often

set goals within a one-year time frame, and we rarely make a conscious choice about which of our goals is most important to us. We
can also find ourselves in pursuit of goals before we've really taken
time to think them through, determine their real cost or consider
what's really important to us.

Maybe you're in the habit of coming home exhausted and turning on the television rather than sitting at the table and sharing
a meal with a loved one or listening to your favourite music or
reading that book you've been longing to get to – or planning the
next year of your life.

After the initial spurt of growing up and becoming an adult, most
of us don't stop to think about goals in the same serious way we did
when we carefully planned our education, our career, our first place
away from our parents. We begin to 'follow our noses', reacting to
circumstances and meeting our immediate needs and the needs of
those around us. All this becomes a full-time job and more.

Time goes by and soon we begin to feel our lives are out of control and there's nothing we can do about it. Things which matter
most to us aren't getting enough attention and life gets frustrating.
We feel we're no longer in charge of our own lives.

In one of my recent 'bibles', Sogyal Rinpoche says,

If we look into our lives, we will see clearly how many unimportant
tasks, so called 'responsibilities' accumulate to fill them up. One master
compares them to 'housekeeping in a dream'. We tell ourselves we want
to spend time on the important things of life, but there never *is* any time.

There are things which have to be done and we feel we have no
choice about it. And by the time we are finished doing everything
that has to be done, we're too tired to think of doing anything else.
Gradually we become cynical about things like New Year's resolutions and Lifetime Goals. Why bother? The thought that we could
actually *do* something about our deepest frustrations just doesn't
occur to us any more. We give up on creating a life that is more

meaningful and fulfilling and settle for what we have. We give up on ourselves and our ability to make things happen.

Yet part of us is unwilling to settle – the part that wakes up in the middle of the night worrying but also contemplating the things that matter most to us: *What am I doing here? What have I really accomplished? Why can't I make better use of my time? What can I do to take better care of my family? When is it going to be my turn? Surely there must be more to life than all these worries and frustrations? What's the point?*

Perhaps you'll be listening to music or watching a play or film – for a time you're lifted out of your busy life and moved to remember who you really are and what you want for yourself and those you love.

And then the music or the play is over and these important questions fade into the background, covered over by ritual doubts and fears. The day takes over, as it always does, and you don't take the time to think about what you really want or how to make it happen if you did.

THE STRONGEST MOTIVATION FOR DOING BEST YEAR YET IS TO FIND THE WAY TO LIVE YOUR LIFE SO IT SHOWS WHAT REALLY MATTERS TO YOU – SO YOU ARE TRUE TO YOURSELF.

Probably you, like many, get frustrated and say '*I've had enough!*' You set a goal and start to do something about making it happen, but then your drive fizzles out. Too often our most important goals are not set with the belief that they can really be achieved, so that before long we lose momentum. We've forgotten how to keep our attention on what we've accomplished rather than on our failures and mistakes. We forget how to live our lives remembering what we do well, and therefore stop building confidence in ourselves and our ability to succeed.

We human beings have an enormous capacity to remember our failures while forgetting our successes. The memory of our failures causes us to lower our sights and lessen our opinion of ourselves. We become frozen in the shadow of our biggest problems and can't turn around to face them. While in parts of our lives we may be strong and capable, we seem to lose potency in the face of those concerns that cause us the most pain.

Here are examples of the kind of problems I'm talking about – many of them have been shared by clients and many I've faced myself:

- *My relationship with my teenage son has gone astray: that brilliant, sparkling little man who used to run and jump on my lap and tell me everything seems lost to me. If I'd let myself think about it too long, I would weep.*
- *The success I've struggled towards for so long is here, but I'm working harder than ever and there's no time to enjoy it. The days go by so quickly and I'm not making the best use of the time I have. The dream for which I sacrificed so much has dissolved.*
- *The body that used to bound up stairs and give me the energy to work and think for hours and hours seems to have run out of steam but there's no time to get it back into shape – probably too late anyway.*
- *I seem to spend most of my time at the office in meetings, handling last-minute emergencies or dealing with other people's problems. I can never seem to get around to sitting back from my job and thinking about the future and how we're going to get ourselves out of some of these messes once and for all.*
- *I want to make my mark, I want my life to matter. How can I find more fulfilment in my job? Should I leave this job and find another one which gives me a better chance to do this? Why don't I devote at least some of my time to causes I care about?*
- *I feel as if I'm chasing my tail most of the time. There's always a deadline to meet and it's always tomorrow. I know I should plan ahead and stop procrastinating as much as I do, but I don't have time!*

- *What's wrong with me? Why isn't there one person in the world to love me and share my life? I don't want to be alone.*
- *I feel stuck in this job – I'm going nowhere fast. They don't realize how good I am and probably never will. But I really don't know how to find something with a better future. I can't figure out what to do, so I do nothing.*
- *Why can't I find some time to 'stop the music' at least once a day to meditate and contemplate and let the noise of the TO DO list be silent for a moment? How do I stop the mental chattering when I do?*
- *What's driving my life – me or my overdraft? Most of my vital spirit and energy is spent in the pursuit of money and I don't know how to get off this merry-go-round of survival.*
- *The person I married years ago who loved me so deeply and hung on my every word is now too busy and preoccupied really to look at me or listen to me. But now I'm so frustrated, angry and resentful that I don't really care whether he does or not.*

The longer we go on putting up with these painful situations and not reclaiming our dreams, the more we diminish in our own eyes and then lose our ability to make the changes which mean the most to us. At some point we stop thinking about the possibility of changing any of it. That's just the way it is, mustn't grumble. The idea of even setting a goal such as *Start enjoying the success I've achieved* or *Put some romance back in my life* or *Find a new job which gives me a chance to prove myself* simply never occurs to us any more.

Sometimes we make promises to ourselves, such as:

- *Tonight I'm going to go home and not touch the television.*
- *This weekend I'll take my son out for a drive and see if I can't begin to get closer to him.*
- *Next Monday the diet starts!*
- *Tonight I'm going to the gym on the way home.*
- *First thing tomorrow I'm going to look in the classifieds and pick*

a few jobs I could go for.
- *On the way home today I'm going to stop and get some flowers and a bottle of wine...*

But too often we don't keep them, and every time this happens we become somehow weaker and believe in ourselves a little bit less.

It is this way we think about ourselves that stops us more than our failure to think ahead or set goals. We come to believe that we're not capable of making the changes that matter, and therefore stop setting goals and planning ahead in any meaningful way. And the life we really want for ourselves drifts out of reach.

OUR LIMITING BELIEFS ABOUT OURSELVES BECOME BRICK WALLS IN FRONT OF US, KEEPING US FROM EVEN THINKING ABOUT HOW TO MAKE THE BIG CHANGES OR SET THE BIG GOALS.

Once we've come to this point in life, we begin to protect ourselves with familiar defences and excuses, such as:

- *Why think about it, I know I can't afford to have what I want anyway.*
- *I'm not willing to sacrifice now for something in the future.*
- *I can't stand the thought of trying and failing one more time.*

And so, while we wouldn't think of getting in a car and not knowing whether we're going to Birmingham or Bournemouth, we gradually become a passenger in our own lives. Years go by and we never get out of the car to see how it's doing and where it's going. We simply sit in the back seat preoccupied by our busy, busy lives, which are moving too fast to allow time to stop the car, take stock, consider alternative routes, or set goals to change direction, if necessary – in short, to get back into the driving seat.

BEST YEAR YET

The Best Year Yet three-hour process forces us to get out of the car and take a better look at ourselves and our lives. *How far have we come? What have we accomplished? What do we do well? What have we learned about travelling? Have we taken any wrong turns? And most importantly, how far have we come?*

This exercise, although not always easy, becomes more of a pleasant and uplifting experience than a painful process of recrimination. It helps us face these important questions and take stock. The biggest challenge is finding three hours in a life where there *is* no time to do this kind of thing. But if we want to be more responsible about creating our lives rather than merely coping with our lot, we must do Best Year Yet *instead* of something else.

This is the most difficult part for most of us. Just don't do that thing you *think* you have to do right now. Do Best Year Yet instead. We've usually held our Best Year Yet courses on a Saturday and it's easy for the people there to realize that in order to come to the course they will have to forgo the weekly laundry, the Saturday errands, cleaning the house, writing letters, paying bills, seeing their friends – or whatever else they usually feel they have to do on a Saturday.

Even though they will have spent the day at the course, they can see that they'll get the clothes washed and somehow get food in the house. Those things always get done. It's not *those* things which are the problem – finding time to plan your life is the problem, but once it's done, it makes far more difference than getting the laundry done. So grab yourself by the collar, get a pen and paper and make yourself sit down and answer the ten questions. Or do what some of the people who have come to the course have done – book three hours with a family member, colleague or friend and do the exercise together.

The process asks you to look back over your past year and then begin to think about next year by asking yourself these *Ten Best Year Yet Questions*:

1. *What did I accomplish?*
2. *What were my biggest disappointments?*
3. *What did I learn?*
4. *How do I limit myself and how can I stop?*
5. *What are my personal values?*
6. *What roles do I play in my life?*
7. *Which role is my major focus for the next year?*
8. *What are my goals for each role?*
9. *What are my top ten goals for the next year?*
10. *How can I make sure I achieve my top ten goals?*

Best Year Yet is very like successful gardening. While I'm not the first person to suggest a strong correlation between life and gardening, think about it for a minute. *We must prepare our soil before we're ready to plant the seeds we want to grow in the next year*. As we answer the first two questions, we look to see what grew and what didn't grow last season. The third question helps us discover what we've learned and what we want to remember for next year.

Reviewing successes and failures in the garden involves little guilt or self-recrimination – a good lesson. We take a moment to enjoy the successes of the past year so we can be strengthened by them rather than weighed down by our failures. In other words, let go of your disappointments and failures – pull them out as you would weed your garden. Why should they crowd the space and negatively influence what happens next year?

The fourth question is the last step before planting. Here we fertilize the soil – enriching every clump by working in the lessons we've learned and the intentions we have for the year ahead. Enriching the earth in your garden means making sure that the way you're thinking about yourself will contribute to your success rather than poison your soil. Imagine what would grow in a garden polluted with a strong sense of failure. The secret of Best Year Yet is planting seeds in rich soil.

TOO OFTEN PEOPLE SET GOALS WITHOUT PREPARING THE PERSONAL ENVIRONMENT FOR THOSE GOALS TO SUCCEED. BEST YEAR YET, REFINED BY SO MANY OVER FOURTEEN YEARS, CLEARLY AND SUCCINCTLY PREPARES THIS ENVIRONMENT.

So the process starts by asking you to think back over the past year of your life and remember what you *did* accomplish and focus on the causes for celebration. Yes, you. This first step allows you to balance your view of the past year and of yourself. It's so easy to remember our failures: promises not kept, times we let others down, New Year's resolutions that didn't last a week, weight not lost, miles not run, mornings we didn't meditate, letters not written, cupboards not cleaned, books not read, friends not seen, lost hours with our children... here our memories are so vivid. We lose sight of the strengths and gifts we do have and then fail to use these gifts to make the changes we want to make. We don't take steps towards the goals that are most important to us because we don't think we can.

Because the problem for all of us is not a lack of ability. It is a matter of focusing the ability we have on things which matter most to us, while at the same time renewing our belief in ourselves.

Reviewing your past successes gives a chance to balance the way you think about yourself and – having learned from your failures – let them go. In this way, as you begin thinking seriously about the year ahead, you are reminded that you *do* have the ability to set and achieve new goals. While it may be uncomfortable to think about yourself in this way, to do so is to know yourself again and begin to feel, as you did at age eight or ten, that you can be the master of your own destiny.

MORE THAN ANYTHING, BEST YEAR YET IS ABOUT STARTING TO
BELIEVE IN YOURSELF AGAIN AND BECOMING MUCH TOUGHER IN
THE FACE OF LIFE'S BIGGEST CHALLENGES. THE APPROACH HELPS
YOU TO USE YOUR COMMON SENSE AND INTELLIGENCE IN NEW WAYS
TO CREATE A HAPPIER LIFE FOR YOURSELF.

I remember Jane Fonda's story of how hard it was for her (she was
then in her mid-forties) to get past her terror and learn to do a back-
flip into a lake for her role in *On Golden Pond*. Her co-star,
Katharine Hepburn, watched her and when, after many days filled
with hours and hours of practising she succeeded, said to her,
'*Everyone should know that feeling of overcoming fear and master-
ing something. People who aren't taught that become soggy.*'

DON'T LET WEEDS GROW AROUND YOUR DREAMS

This quote from H. Jackson Brown's *Life's Little Instruction Book*
is one of my favourites and reminds me of people I know who have
followed Ms Hepburn's advice. I'd like to tell you about a few of
the friends and clients who have had the courage, heart and discipline to use the lessons of Best Year Yet in their lives.

It all sounds a bit glib and easy when their lives are reduced to
such short 'success stories' as the ones which follow, but if we can
move past that point of view we can see how each in their own way
decided to make a change in something that was important to them.
Also, take note if you find it much harder to believe these experiences than the earlier examples of people's problems.

The woman who had left her husband for a confirmed bach-
elor. However, six months later he stopped telling her how
much he cared for her; it had been five weeks since he'd said
he loved her and she was afraid she'd made a big mistake.
When she realized her focus was not on the result she wanted
but rather her fear, she set a goal to *Develop a great relation-*

ship with Sam and learn to remember how much I am loved.

She was able to keep this focus and dissolve her fears; within a year they were married.

The highly successfully entrepreneur in his late fifties who wanted to move on to something new and more exciting but felt guilty leaving the loyal people in the company he'd built up over the past 20 years – and was worried that, at his age, he could not really afford to go out on his own. His goal: *Finish with my company and be ready to launch my new venture by the beginning of the year.*

He found and developed a new person whom he trusted with his company and his people. Now that he's moved on and started his new business, he's filled with new enthusiasm and energy for what he's doing.

The woman who, having spent her life taking care of her five children and supporting her husband's career, longed to find a way to express herself and be more creative in her life, but who had long ago lost the confidence to figure out how to do it. Her goal: *Find a way to build a successful business which allows me to express my sense of style and creativity.*

It took her a while to identify what type of business she wanted and how to get started when she did. But finally she opened a shop selling the kind of jewellery and clothing she wore and loved.

The talented journalist who was earning a small weekly wage as a television critic for a national daily newspaper and struggling with a ten-month old daughter, a huge mortgage and growing anxiety. She found that she never liked doing things she was afraid of and was afraid of pursuing what she wanted most. Her goal: *Build a career doing what I love to do which pays me what I'm really worth.*

She approached the project of her personal transformation with great determination and intelligence. It didn't happen overnight but she worked steadily and consciously and today is a best-selling author currently working on her sixth book.

The couple who had worked together for years to grow a successful business which now kept them overly busy and exhausted doing work neither one of them enjoyed. When early in the recession the bank put on intense pressure, they felt the burden of the business more than ever. Out of a strong sense of duty and a good deal of fear, they were both continuing to invest a lot of money and time in the growth of the business when that was the last thing they wanted for themselves. Their goal: *Move on to a working life that is more satisfying, creative and rewarding for both of us – and make this move as soon as possible.*

Once they allowed themselves to set the goal they really wanted, the business began to turn around and they found a friendly buyer so they could back out and set off on their own again.

The successful Managing Director who had begun to feel like an old man before the age of 50 because of severe back and leg pain which kept him from doing much that he loved. He was deeply depressed because he felt like a prisoner in his own body; he was used to being able to pursue a wide range of business and personal interests without such restriction. His goal: *Feel physically, mentally and emotionally free to live my life as I choose.*

He pursued this goal with relentless discipline, attacking it from many angles – medical, emotional, mental – and within months was walking straighter and moving without pain.

The couple who had suffered severe money problems for years – both actors, it had become harder and harder for them to get work. They had been forced to sell their home and move to a smaller one; soon they feared they would have to take their children out of the school that meant so much to them. At the beginning of the year, they made a strong commitment to *Put money problems behind us once and for all.*

Their approach was relentless, calling on friends for support and talking with experts to help them get things sorted. Within a couple of months one of them was offered a major role in an international television series.

The young woman who had left nursing for a sales job in order to make more money and better use of her skills, but who had just finished a year when she hadn't achieved her sales target. She was concerned she might lose her job now that the recession had really hit her company. Her goal: *Make this my breakthrough year.*

Even though it was the toughest year the company had ever known, she started shifting her perception of herself and doing things she'd previously not tried. By the end of the year she had cracked her target and became Salesperson of the Year. She has now been promoted to Client Services Director for the business and is using the same people skills that made her a good nurse to manage people in a business setting.

The designer who was doing well in her career but who was miserable in a relationship where she was comfortable but which she felt she had probably outgrown. She desperately wanted to get married and have children, but with this man? She was afraid that if she let this one go, she might not find the one she really wanted. Her goal: *Move on and find the man I'm going to marry.*

She found the courage to end her relationship and move out

on her own. Although uncertain, she kept her eye on the goal and eventually met a bright young barrister with whom she could develop a much stronger bond; they married and now have two beautiful daughters.

Behind each of these people is an ordinary person who found the courage to act – to face the big challenges and make their dreams come true. They built the inner strength to stop worrying about their problems and direct their focus towards the goal they wanted to achieve. They took the time to step back from the busy-ness of life and all its issues to put their attention on the goal which, when achieved, would make the most difference to them. And they did their best to avoid the pitfalls of explanation, complaint and excuse so they could keep going until they got what they wanted.

PUTTING MY BEST YEAR YET IN WRITING

As we've said many times so far, it's such a challenge to set serious goals about things which really matter. If you're reading this book then you'll know I've finally been successful in achieving my goal of writing a book, a dream I've had for as long as I can remember. But nothing happened about this goal for years and years and years. In fact, even though I've been doing Best Year Yet for myself since 1981, it didn't make it to my list of Top Ten Goals until now. It just seemed an impossible dream to me so I didn't give it any serious thought. Much longing, mind you, but no serious thought.

And even though I was leading Best Year Yet courses and coaching others to have their big dreams come true, this goal lay dormant and untouched beneath a pile of regret and resentment. There was always a reason why now wasn't the time:

- *I'm too tired at the end of the day and on the weekends.*
- *My business partners and clients need me to be doing something more important and far more urgent.*

- *The onset of menopause has stopped my brain functioning.*
- *My writing a book wouldn't contribute to the direction we want the business to go.*
- *It would be a waste of time doing something that probably wouldn't earn us any money.*

... and on and on.

The thread you can see running through my reasons for not writing is the mindset *'I'm a victim of circumstances beyond my control.'* A common theme for me and certainly one I've often spotted in other people. Over the years the tune in my head was the same, though the key changed from time to time: *I'd love to write. I'm probably a great writer. I really have something to say but I can't because...* (fill in the blank from the list above).

Several years ago I even subscribed to a magazine for writers with the hope that it would stimulate me to do something, but every month when another issue arrived on the doormat I was filled with guilt and frustration. I piled them in a neat chronological stack by my bed so that 'when the time came' I could read them, learn about writing and motivate myself to get started. But that time never came.

Until one New Year's Day, that is, when Tim and I spent the day with our friends, Jock and Susie.

At some point we were talking about Best Year Yet and I was scribbling down the ten questions for them to use, explaining how the process worked and telling them about the good time we'd had doing the exercise a couple of days before with our son Jeff, who was with us during his Christmas break from university. (He'd started the exercise with little enthusiasm as he listed four accomplishments and 26 disappointments! But later he told us how good it felt having let go of some of the terrible memories he had of the term just gone. *'That's done. I need to move on.'*)

Then one of them said, *You know, you really should write a book about this!* We laughed at the tired suggestion; we know each other well and sometimes tease each other about dreams gone mouldy.

Mine is the well-known book. But somehow they got through to me that day and I began to get excited about writing in a way that was different for me. I felt that they really did want me to write the book and they convinced me that Best Year Yet was an important idea that could help a lot of people. Music to my ears. And so I started to believe in myself more seriously, redid my goals for the year (changing No 4 on my list of Top Ten Goals to: *Write my first book and find a fabulous agent and publisher*).

And when I next spoke to Jeff, he looked at me with his smirk and said, '*Yeah, Mom, just do it!*'

After my initial euphoria, however, I came up against another stack of limiting beliefs:

- *I'm probably not nearly as good as I think I am.*
- *Every book I want to write has already been written.*
- *I can't stand the thought of people reading what I've written – they'll probably laugh at me behind my back and never tell me.*
- *This is all so trite and stupid and redundant.*
- *How can anyone be expected to write a book when they're already working 50–60 hours a week?*
- *No publisher will want to publish anything I've written anyway.*

All this with a husband who kept encouraging me to write a book, telling me how he knew it would be a best-seller.

WE LOVE OUR LIMITATIONS! WE MUST – BECAUSE WE CERTAINLY DON'T WANT TO LET THEM GO.

VICTIM OF CIRCUMSTANCE?

Most of us become comfortable thinking of ourselves as smaller than our problems, feeling a victim of circumstances and blaming others for the fact we don't have what we want. It's not that other people aren't horrid sometimes, but becoming their victim makes us powerless. Hopefully it's easy for you to see how my blaming other people and situations for not being able to write my book robbed me of this goal for years. I had made myself impotent. And yet it's just a smaller example of something we can see around us everywhere.

There is always someone and something to blame in our lives. It becomes a habit and not an easy one for any of us to give up. It's a comfortable old friend. Just yesterday I asked my friend Mary if she'd heard a weather forecast for the coming weekend. *'No I haven't,'* she said, *'but I'm going to the country to visit my aunt and her family. The prediction is for the weather to be beautiful, but with my luck it'll probably rain.'* What luck? Who says? How crazy to wallow in the perverse satisfaction of such statements, whose empty reward is being able to say, *'See I knew it!'* or *'I told you so.'* We can hear evidence of this attitude everywhere if we listen for it, but we're so used to it we're largely unaware of it or its cost. Catching ourselves in this self-defeating approach to life, as I had to do with my writing, is the only way out.

Too rarely do we hear anyone say,

- *This weekend is going to be great!*
- *Leave it to me, I'll deal with it.*
- *I'm sorry, it's my fault. It won't happen again.*
- *We've made a couple of mistakes but we'll keep going until we get it right.*

The alternative to playing the victim is to become tougher in ourselves and start taking personal responsibility for our own lives.

I understand how hard it can be. But Best Year Yet works and it goes on working year after year, dream after dream. Especially for me as I sit here tapping away on my computer, enjoying the process of passing it on.

As far as I can tell, life is more about learning than anything, and again and again I learn the lesson of the Chinese proverb which tells us that *'If we don't change our direction, we are likely to end up where we are going.'*

READY OR NOT?

By now you've read quite a bit about me and people I've known. Now it's time to take a moment to think about yourself. The more aware you can be of yourself as you begin this process, the more successful you'll be. Answer the following questions as honestly as you can. No one's watching:

LIFE SO FAR

Circle either T or F, depending on whether the statement is true or false for you:

T F There have been times in my life when I have set and achieved goals.

T F When I take the time to think about it, I'm proud of what I've accomplished so far.

T F While I feel I have much to be grateful for, something is missing and I'd like to find out what it is.

T F I know I have more potential than I've used so far.

T F I can remember times in the past when I kept going regardless and made something happen.

T F I know that I've lost confidence in myself over the years, but I'm not quite ready to give up.

T F I know that if I tackled at least one or two of the issues which trouble me most, I'd be much happier.

T F I find it easier to remember my failures than my successes and I see how this has caused me to stop believing in myself as strongly as I once did.

T F It troubles me that although I have strong personal beliefs and values, the way I've lived my life so far hasn't reflected these as much as I'd like.

You don't have to be a rocket scientist to figure out that the more 'T's you have circled, the better chance you have to succeed in setting plans and making them happen. How many did you circle?

PERSONAL BELIEFS AND VALUES

Tick those statements which express your personal beliefs and values:

- ❏ I am responsible for myself and what happens to me.
- ❏ Although I sometimes resist the idea, I'm aware that even a bit more discipline could make a big difference in my life.
- ❏ I believe that anything is possible if you set your mind to it.
- ❏ *As ye sow, so shall ye reap* – or *what goes around comes around*.
- ❏ Keeping a positive attitude is vital to my success.
- ❏ It's wise to ask for help when I need it.
- ❏ It's all right to make mistakes because it shows I'm trying.
- ❏ The more successful I am, the more important it is to give back in some way.
- ❏ I'm committed to the happiness of my loved ones.
- ❏ It's very important to me to live up to my personal beliefs and values.

Obviously in this section the information is personal and there are no right or wrong answers. However, I believe most of these statements would be recognized by people who have become truly successful. What matters most is to know what *you* believe in and what *you* value.

Our sense that something is missing comes at those times when we're off the course set by our beliefs and values. One of the Ten Best Year Yet questions explores this area more fully.

WHAT MOTIVATES MOST OF US FAR MORE THAN MATERIAL SUCCESS OR RECOGNITION IS OUR DESIRE TO BE TRUE TO OURSELVES AND LIVE OUR LIVES IN WAYS THAT DEMONSTRATE OUR PERSONAL VALUES AND BELIEFS.

EXCUSES I HAVE KNOWN AND LOVED

Tick the ones you've used in the past. I really want to do things differently, but I can't because...

❏ I want to keep my options open.
❏ Once something's gone bad, you can't really change it.
❏ Goal-setting and thinking about what I want is such a selfish and self-absorbed business.
❏ I passed my 'sell-by' date a long time ago.
❏ Once I get through this busy patch, I'm really going to take time to sort myself out.
❏ It's boring to know where I'm going and what's going to happen next.
❏ If I fix my mind on a goal, I'll miss other exciting opportunities when they present themselves.
❏ You can't teach an old dog new tricks.
❏ I can't be bothered.

To be honest, I'd be suspicious of anyone who didn't tick most of these excuses. Welcome to the human race. The challenge for all of us is to become more aware of the times we're using these excuses rather than doing what we want to do to move ourselves forward. Be especially wary of those which you see as statements of truth rather than excuses. They have the power to stop you.

HOW MOTIVATED AM I?

On a scale of 1–10, with 10 being the highest, rate yourself on the following:

_____ I am committed to making positive change in my life.
_____ Planning a year ahead and setting goals for myself makes sense to me. I'm ready to give it a try.
_____ I can count on myself to do what I need to do this time.
_____ I know a great deal about what I need to do to change my life.

_____ It matters to me that I live up to my personal beliefs and values.

_____ I'm willing to do whatever it takes to make this process work for me.

_____ There are other people in my life who would benefit if I took the time to plan the next year of my life.

_____ Even though I'm afraid to confront some of my problems, I'm ready to do it.

_____ I'm now ready to use my abilities and my intelligence more fully and courageously.

_____ I'm going to set aside three hours in the next week to answer the Ten Best Year Yet questions. No matter what.

_____ **TOTAL SCORE**

Total your score on motivation and refer to the chart below to see how ready you are for your Best Year Yet.

90–100 Congratulations. It's possible that life will never again be the same for you.

70–89 Although you may need to push yourself from time to time, you could be on your way to your Best Year Yet.

51–69 Hard to tell what's going to happen. You're not quite sure whether you're really ready to get in the driving seat.

If your score is below 50, you've just told yourself that you're not ready to make the most of the information in this book. Either improve your approach or wait until you're feeling more confident. However, any of you who scored a 10 on the last statement has the best chance of all.

JUST DO IT

In over 20 years of working with people, I've seen one big difference between those who truly succeed in making things happen and the ones who don't: those who do, act.

They think of an idea and they move on it. They get a feeling that something really could work and they take the steps to try it out. They take a course and they find the discipline to put what they've learned into practice. They read a book, find an idea they like and they take steps to use it in their lives. They hear about a meditation that could decrease their stress level and give them a stronger sense of who they really are and they set aside the time and get started. They just do it.

So if you're one of these people, stop now and turn to Part Three where you'll find the Best Year Yet Workshop. Make a cup of coffee or pour a glass of wine, turn on some music and start writing your answers. It's that simple. And three hours from now you'll know even more about where you're going and feel more motivated to get there. Just make yourself do it – the way you usually do.

According to Dr Stephen Covey, the first habit of highly effective people is to BE PROACTIVE. In other words, rather than letting life happen to you, make it happen. Even if you don't recognize yourself as one of those people who just does it, you could *become* one of them simply by moving straight to the questions and getting started on *your* Best Year Yet.

Some people are born to 'just do it' – they seem to have come packaged with a strong inner drive or compulsion to succeed and they move full steam ahead regardless. But most of us have had to learn a great deal in order to do a better job designing our own lives; we were made rather than born. I'm certainly one of these. Compared to the consciousness with which I now live my life, I spent most of my early days in a sleepy fog, feeling jerked around by life but '*doing my best given the circumstances*'.

So, even if you're not one of the high-driven people, you're not out of the race. You've already achieved so much in your life and I hope you appreciate that about yourself. But in order to make the best use of this book you need the necessary discipline to sit down and write your answers to the ten questions.

THE TRUTH IS, YOU ALREADY KNOW A GREAT DEAL – MORE THAN YOU THINK YOU KNOW – ABOUT WHAT TO DO TO CHANGE YOUR LIFE FOR THE BETTER.

The trick is doing it, taking that first step, making it happen. And yet often we don't. While it's important to find out what stops you and why (which we'll explore in later chapters) what works best is just getting on with it. Understanding your limitations can come later.

Answering the ten deceptively simple but powerful Best Year Yet questions can make all the difference. It's not always an easy exercise, but in the process of answering the questions you'll learn a lot about yourself, how you make things happen and how you hold yourself back. You'll begin to see how to build a more meaningful life for yourself and soon you'll be looking forward to the year ahead. Promise. Just do it.

ONE MORE WORD ABOUT GETTING ON WITH IT: IF YOU'RE WONDERING, *IS THIS BOOK THE ONE WHICH WILL REALLY HELP ME?* – THE ANSWER IS IT CERTAINLY COULD BE. IT'S UP TO YOU. AS YOU WELL KNOW, IT'S NOT ENOUGH TO BUY THE BOOK. IN ORDER TO STOP FLOATING FROM ONE RESOLUTION TO ANOTHER OR DRIFTING FROM ONE GOOD INTENTION TO THE NEXT, YOU NEED TO ACT.

Most of us trap ourselves by not being willing to take the necessary steps to be the master of our own lives, yet we'll be damned if we'll let anyone or anything serve as our master in the meantime! The result – no one's in charge. We get nowhere. Every bit of true progress I've made in my life has come from really listening to a teacher or an author and having the discipline to practise his or her lessons until I have learned them. Action and follow-through are everything.

There's another prevalent mindset that can stop us making the best use of the modern repackaging of ancient wisdom so popular in the past ten to fifteen years: cynicism. Labelling any discipline of self-improvement or personal transformation *silly ineffectual nonsense* or *psycho-babble* and displaying a general snobbery towards anyone who tries to support us in making positive change in our lives is just another path of avoidance which stops us doing what we want to do. I know, I thought this way for years.

So, if you've decided that this book could help you and you're ready to get going straight away, stop reading and turn to the questions and get started. Or if you are someone who prefers the more deliberate approach, that works too, sometimes better. This book is not about the quick-fix or creating overnight miracles, although for some of you it might be. Whoever you are, if you feel there are changes you'd like to make and you scored well on motivation, now is the time. Just do it!

PART TWO

THE TEN BEST YEAR YET QUESTIONS

WHAT DID I ACCOMPLISH?

Increasing your self-esteem is easy.
Simply do good things
and remember that you did them.

JOHN-ROGER

THE GOOD NEWS

No one's looking. Start to tell yourself what you feel good about. Maybe no one noticed some of your finest moments, but *you* did. Make a note. Maybe others did notice – those count, too.

- *Did you get through another year of school? What were the best times?*
- *Did you move house? Did you decorate or repair the one you have? Did you have a good clear out? Did you take things to Oxfam?*
- *Did you start a new job or get a promotion? Have you been doing a better job at work? What deserves a pat on the back?*
- *How much money did you earn in the last year? Did you pay off some of your debts? Did you manage to put some more in the deposit account?*
- *Did you get married? Have a child? Did one or more of your*

*children have a good year, get over a rough patch? Have you been
a better parent this year?*

- *Did you finally start to get fit? Are you exercising even a little
more? How do your clothes feel compared to the beginning of the
year – a little looser? Have you started to eat more healthily?*
- *Have you been in touch with old friends more this year? Did you
make some new ones? Have you been a better friend to the ones
you have?*
- *Did you start to do more enjoyable things? Concerts? Reading?
Theatre? Films? Seeing friends?*
- *Are you doing a better job of keeping in touch with absent family
members and friends?*

Even if some of these questions don't spark memories of your best
moments, force yourself to think about your achievements and
times when you were proud of yourself, did something well or put
a problem behind you. Make a note. Bragging is allowed.

WHEN YOU FIND ACHIEVEMENTS TO CELEBRATE, YOU NOURISH
YOUR SPIRIT AND MOTIVATE YOURSELF.

I'm not asking you to invent something but merely to notice what
you *did* achieve and then write a list of the good news for the past
year. Think about the headlines, but get beyond that – everything
counts, big and little. Look at the sample list at the end of this
chapter, which illustrates how important it is to remember as much
as you can about what you've achieved.

Use this experience to get closer to a new part of yourself – the
strong inner part that really keeps you going day after day. It may
be uncomfortable – most of us are much more at home with our
failures. So much easier to talk with friends about things which
aren't going well, to have a good moan. But the stretch into new
territory is worth it.

There's nothing phoney about this – what we're talking about here goes beyond mere 'positive thinking'. Positive thinking is too often the same as papering over the cracks and pretending things are different than they are. That's not what we're doing. As you answer these questions, be absolutely honest with yourself. No one else need ever see what you've written – you're safe. Whatever happened last year, tell the truth. Just don't get stuck thinking it was far worse than it was, remembering the struggles while forgetting the triumphs.

Rebalance your perception of yourself. I'm asking you to realize that the truth is far better news than you've been letting yourself believe. You're laying the groundwork for your Best Year Yet; if you start by thinking about the good news, you'll be in far better shape to make it happen. I'm asking you to be responsible for how good you are and to put the whip away!

Yes, it would be wonderful if others noticed how good you are and how well you're doing. But that's not yet the world we're living in. So, as a first step, do it for yourself and then you'll be much more willing and able to do it for others.

WHY START WITH ACCOMPLISHMENTS?

The first question of Best Year Yet leads you in a positive direction and gives you the chance to re-balance your perception of yourself and what you've achieved in the past year. Almost without exception, people's initial thoughts about the past are negative. An invisible magnet draws us to the bad news. Unless we stop to think about what really happened, we assume that there is far greater cause for disappointment than celebration.

Rarely do we stop and think about what we've achieved in a day, let alone a year. Imagine that you've started a day by making a TO DO list of everything you need to do. Say the list is ten items long and at the end of the day you've achieved eight out of ten. Do you say 'Well, done' or even 'Not bad'? Good for you – but most of us just feel guilty that we didn't achieve _the other two_. Our consciousness is snared by the bad news, the things we didn't get done. Again our self-esteem diminishes and we're probably not looking forward to the next day as a result.

This is no accident. We live in a world inhabited by people doing the same. Well-meaning friends and relatives can have a negative slant on things, and it becomes embarrassing to be positive or optimistic. We're told that bad news sells newspapers and attracts more television viewers. We live in a negative culture which focuses on the bad news, so it's easy to make an unconscious assumption that there's *more* of it. But that's not the case.

Most people find when they answer this question that they're pleasantly surprised to remember how much they have achieved over the past year. Rather than a few meagre achievements in a field of failures, it's often the opposite. We start here so that you can see this for yourself and be energized and uplifted by this perspective of yourself.

AWARENESS BRINGS ITS OWN REWARD. SHIFTING YOUR ATTENTION TO WHAT YOU *HAVE* ACCOMPLISHED IN THE PAST YEAR AWAKENS YOUR CAN DO! ATTITUDE AND GETS YOU BACK IN TOUCH WITH YOUR ABILITY TO MAKE THINGS HAPPEN.

In this way you'll see the past in a new light and start to rebalance the effects of your environment – that of your own making as well as the wider one in which you live. Your own accomplishments are the best and most authentic reminder that you *can* create your own future and become more the master of your own destiny.

So Best Year Yet starts with a pat on the back.

HOW DID WE GET THIS WAY?

But where did it all begin? How did we learn to be so much more critical than positive?

I believe we were carefully taught from the time we were small. Not by a carefully-conceived curriculum designed to teach us to whip ourselves mentally and emotionally – to flog ourselves for what we haven't done, for mistakes we make, for our failure to achieve a higher standard of performance and behaviour. No one set out to create a population so hard on themselves that they feel incapable of making important changes in their lives. Nevertheless the impact of parents, teachers and, as we grow older, bosses and others has been as effective as if they had planned it all.

Of course the bad news is that many of us *are* parents, teachers or bosses – and some (like me) have been all three. Most of us are victims and perpetrators at the same time. So I make these points with a great deal of humility and compassion for each of us and for whatever drives us to interact with others in any way that leaves them feeling smaller or less able. Few of us want this outcome as a result of our interactions with our children, our friends, our students or our employees. Yet in spite of the best of intentions, the messages we give and receive are far more negative than positive. Most parents spend far more time telling children what _not_ to do than what _to_ do; they have developed a habit (probably through being the children of their own parents) of correcting far more than praising. We are carefully taught the sin of pride and of feeling good about something we've achieved.

While I'm not recommending that we walk down the street with our chest puffed out letting everyone know *'I'm the greatest!'*, we need to do something to stop operating with this unbalanced view of ourselves which robs us of our spirit and our belief in ourselves. The effect of this phenomenon reaches every part of our lives. So while feeling better about ourselves is a private matter, it's also a vital one. But it's not easy.

Even as I sit here writing this book, making all these wise points, I often catch myself being scolded by the negative little voice inside my head: *'This is interesting stuff but you're way behind. You should be getting a lot more written today,'* or *'Why go back and rewrite that paragraph? You're just avoiding moving on to the parts you haven't written.'* or *'This is OK – at least you'll have an interesting Christmas present to give your family next year even though no one else will read it.*' I've learned by now that this little voice is so strongly programmed that it may go on until the day I die. But my job is to flick it away and keep encouraging myself with more accurate and empowering messages, such as '*You're doing fine. This is going to be great, just keep going.*' At the end of the day, maybe only a handful of people will read this, but if I'd listened to this negative little voice I'd have stopped writing and would never know.

The cost of this 'negative conditioning' is enormous. What motivates you more – a correction or a compliment? Which boss do you want to work for – one who constantly points out the error of your ways or one who spends time noticing what you're doing right? If you're like me, the answer is apparent. Running in the first London Marathon, I'll never forget the difference in my reaction to the messages we received from supporters along the way. '*Keep going, don't stop now!*' made me angry, while '*Great job. You're brilliant!*' made me feel like a star.

Obviously we want to be told when we need to improve or have failed to perform to the required standard. Bosses wouldn't be doing their jobs if they failed to do so. But we need far more than this if we're going to do our best and feel like bringing *all* of ourselves to the office in the morning as well as to the business of directing our own lives.

I like visual models to explain concepts and give an easy reminder of important lessons. The Cycle of Productivity opposite demonstrates the flow of four phases of activity – from the time we first think of doing something through to the moment we've finished it.

Cycle of Productivity

4. Acknowledge/
Praise

1. Create/
Decide/Start

3. Complete/
Finish

2. Do/Act

The first of the four segments is the beginning, when we come up with the idea and then decide to do it and get started.

The second section of the Cycle involves the greatest amount of time – this is the period when we're actually doing all that needs to be done to carry out the idea step by step.

The third section is challenging for many – this is the phase where we do the last thing to finish the project or bring the idea to fruition. We tie up all the loose ends so we can say – 'That's it, I did it! Nothing more to do.'

Usually we get stuck in one of the first three segments. There are those who seem to stop at the starting gate. We have lots and lots of ideas but rarely get them off the ground. Or we have far more ideas than we could ever carry out and don't take the time to decide which ones are non-starters and toss them out. So they sit on a list or nag in our minds, making us feel guilty.

Some of us get stuck in the second phase – doing, doing, doing – neither fully completing nor taking ourselves back to the drawing board to create new possibilities. You can recognize this in yourself by the piles of paper, post, magazines, books, crafts in progress and so on, which surround you.

If you're one who slows down in the third segment, you find it difficult to finish anything. As a result there are many incomplete projects in your life. You may have made a good start on a book, a sweater, cleaning out your car or desk drawers, decorating... but what have you *finished* lately?

Obviously, wherever we get stuck it slows us down, getting in our way both mentally and emotionally.

But by far the most important lesson of the Cycle of Productivity comes in segment four. Too many of us simply go straight from the end of the third segment back to the starting line, without taking a pause for acknowledgment, pats on the back, thinking about what happened or learning from it. Our eye is always on what's next or what isn't yet completed, and before long we feel as if we're running on fumes – below the empty mark! We forget to stop for petrol. We don't feel like we're getting anywhere and there's little satisfaction.

This model reminds us to take time to appreciate what we've accomplished and how far we've come. In this way, when we get back to the starting line, whether it's a big new challenge or just tomorrow's TO DO list, we feel more energized and positive and work more productively than ever. We feel far more energetic and the momentum picks up again.

PRAISE AND APPRECIATION FOR THE GOOD NEWS MAKE ALL THE DIFFERENCE. WE FEEL STRONGER AND MORE NATURALLY MOTIVATED AND THERE'S LESS OF THAT NEEDY PART OF US, ALWAYS TRYING TO PROVE OURSELVES AND HOPING SOMEONE WILL NOTICE.

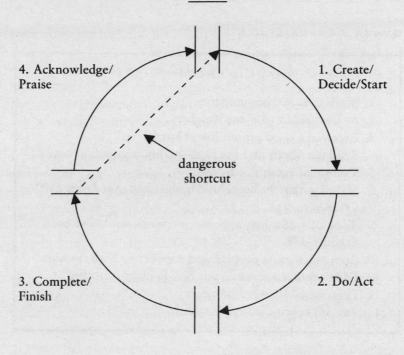

That's why the first question in your Best Year Yet process asks you to remember your accomplishments.

OTHER'S EXPERIENCES

WHAT DID I ACCOMPLISH?

1. Made over 300 hot dinners.
2. At least didn't gain any weight.
3. Received a good promotion at work.
4. Read ten novels and five high-quality non-fiction books.
5. Decorated Sarah's bedroom.
6. Stayed within the household budget and saved over £300.
7. Learned to type.
8. Took care of things at home and work while I've been exhausted.
9. Been much more positive and supportive with the kids.
10. Didn't throw a fit when our holiday was cancelled.
11. Entertained friends a bit more.
12. Paid off credit card every month.

Above is an example of a woman who looks as if she's had a challenging year, yet as you can see she has also been able to put some of her memories in the context of accomplishments.

Several of my clients have been able to look back on some of the toughest years of the recession and remind themselves how well they did considering how horrendous it was. They still named each year their best year because of the amount of personal growth they achieved while changing gears and learning new skills to deal with new circumstances.

After a difficult year it's even more important to acknowledge and appreciate yourself. Focus your outlook on the bright side. We can define our life in any way we choose, regardless of what happens. The challenge is to live life in the context of gratitude instead of complaint.

WHAT WERE MY BIGGEST DISAPPOINTMENTS?

Mistakes are
the portals of discovery.

JAMES JOYCE

THE BAD NEWS

So, what were your disappointments in the past year? Take your pen and write them all down. Remember the times you disappointed yourself and didn't do what you had hoped to do. Recall the instances when others didn't do what you wanted them to do.

- *What dreams didn't come true?*
- *What expectations weren't fulfilled?*
- *Did you want a pay rise? a promotion? a new job?*
- *Did you promise to get yourself out of debt only to get in deeper?*
- *Were you hoping to find a new man or woman in your life?*
- *Did you want to get married to the person you're with but it didn't happen?*
- *Were you hoping for the birth of a child?*
- *Did you lose a loved one either to separation or death?*
- *Do your clothes fit the same or even a bit tighter? Did you start an*

exercise programme and let it lapse and now find yourself disgusted with the way you feel?

- *Did someone who was kind and loving turn off the tap unexpectedly?*
- *Were you hoping for a great holiday only to see the plans change?*
- *Were you hoping to go to school?*
- *Did you hope for a bit more time to yourself? to read? to meditate? to paint? to write? to think? to stare into space?*
- *What else?*

There's more value than you can imagine in just writing these disappointments down. While it seems something to avoid – who wants to think about all this? – I've always felt a great weight lift from me when I gave myself time to think about what happened rather than pretending it didn't hurt so much.

TELLING THE TRUTH TO YOURSELF PROVIDES A GREAT RELEASE, AND DOING IT INSIDE THE BEST YEAR YET CONTEXT SHOWS US THE WAY AHEAD.

Some of us are more comfortable with our failures than with our successes, so we keep them around like cosy old friends. We sometimes feel that the answer to the second question in Best Year Yet is the _real story_, while the successes are a bit contrived. Again, that's not the case.

For others, it's probably necessary to move out of the comfort zone and tell yourself the truth about your disappointments and failures in this way. In any case the rewards for doing so are great.

Don't forget that our view of ourselves has become unbalanced. While answering the first question about accomplishments, you had to go through the discomfort of congratulating yourself. You now have to accept the fact that your failures are not really an accurate reflection of who you are and what you're capable of. (You'll have the chance to explore more of this dynamic in depth when you answer the fourth question, 'How Do I Limit Myself and How Can I Stop?')

And watch out for another pitfall: I've listed five accomplishments, but there are 18 disappointments on my list. See! I am a failure! It doesn't matter in the least. Don't add meaning and significance to what's happened in the past. That's just a good way to attract more of the same so you can be right about how inadequate you are. Avoid the lifetime pursuit of arguing for your limitations. Learn to stop invalidating your accomplishments and focusing on your failures.

Think about it: Who do you know who achieves everything on their list? Who do you know who achieves every goal they set? Do you know anyone who knows anyone who does? Have you read about or heard about anyone who lived without failure or disappointment?

WHAT HAPPENS, HAPPENS. THE ONLY THING WE CAN CONTROL IS HOW WE RESPOND TO WHAT HAPPENS TO US. THE SUCCESSES ARE GREAT AND WE CAN ENJOY THEM. AND THE FAILURES ARE, WELL, GREAT CHARACTER-BUILDERS.

PULL THE WEEDS

You can't grow the way you want if you don't pull the weeds of your disappointments and failures. Certainly we can't avoid them, but once they've grown we must clear them away in order to make room for something new. Answering this question helps us do this.

Looking at your disappointments and letting them go can move you to a place where your self assessment is no longer based primarily on failure – you can start to heal yourself mentally and emotionally, just as you heal yourself physically when you are ill.

But to answer this question you must tell the truth. I don't mean that you have to walk around telling people about how badly you've done, but tell the truth to yourself – that's the important thing. You may have been hiding your failures from yourself for some time. If so, this is a good chance to stop doing that. What we hide from, runs us.

For the purpose of your Best Year Yet exercise, you don't have to tell others about your shortcomings, although at some point you may want to talk with someone in order to pull the weeds in your relationship with them. But for me I find that it's enough just to write everything down, absolutely everything, so that I can get it out of my system. I've never shown my entire list of disappointments to anyone in the fourteen years I've been doing this, but it's made all the difference just to get them down on paper.

EXCESS BAGGAGE

Letting yourself get weighed down with a sense of failure and hopelessness is excess baggage in your life. You don't need it and it's harmful because it makes life difficult and robs you of your ability to move as quickly as you'd like – just as if you were carrying around a couple of heavy suitcases.

And the joke's on all of us. No one else can see your excess baggage, yet there's an unconscious assumption that all your limitations are obvious. But nobody can see your mental movie of the past and the spin you've put on it. They simply don't know your version of history, and those who do are probably far more charitable and respectful of you than you are of yourself.

Remember the times when you've heard friends or colleagues bemoaning their failures or talking about how difficult it is to have what they want? Sometimes it's hard to be sympathetic because you can't understand why they don't just *do* it. You see them as capable and talented people and it's difficult to see what's stopping them.

But what's stopping them, more effectively than a brick wall would, is their excess baggage. They're dragging it into the present and letting it dissolve their sense of what's possible in the future.

We make our excess baggage even heavier by adding negative emotions – anger, resentment, regret, sadness and so on. Of course, these are understandable and human responses, but when they cause you to feel less able than you are – or worse, a victim of circumstances – you get stuck. The downward spiral begins and can degenerate into the kind of bitterness that erodes your character and leads to keeping a mental 'crime log' on others, your circumstances and your environment. Woe is me, yes. But what good does it do you?

> WHAT HAPPENED, HAPPENED. THE BEST YOU CAN DO FOR YOURSELF IS TO EXAMINE WHAT HAPPENED AND THEN DO EVERYTHING YOU CAN TO NEUTRALIZE YOUR EXPERIENCE. GET RID OF THE EXTRA WEIGHT THAT COMES FROM THE NEGATIVE EMOTION. SAVE YOURSELF. STOP CARRYING ALL THAT WEIGHT AROUND. LIGHTEN YOUR LOAD AND LIGHTEN UP.

You can get rid of the negative filter through which you view the world and yourself. You've been walking around wearing a pair of spectacles in need of a good cleaning. Letting yourself answer this question fully helps to clear your vision and enables you to see things as they are. I'll talk more at length about this concept in Chapter Four, *'How Do I Limit Myself and How Can I Stop?'*, but the first step is to take a look at the past year of your life and examine the disappointments you've experienced.

THE PAST

In my Grandma's house there was a wooden sliding door between the lounge and the dining room. When we pulled the brass handles, the two halves of the door came together, separating the two rooms. Imagine yourself standing in front of that closed doorway. The panel on your left is your past and the panel on your right is your future. Most often this is the way we view our lives.

Not much space for the present moment – a thin line but no view – because our minds are so full of the past and the future. The secret of happiness is to open a crack between the past and the future and live life in the moment we're in. Every time I've been able to achieve this, I have a sense of freedom and flow. But how do you do it? How can you get your guilt about the past and your anxiety about the future out of your face long enough to have a renewed sense of yourself in *this* moment in time?

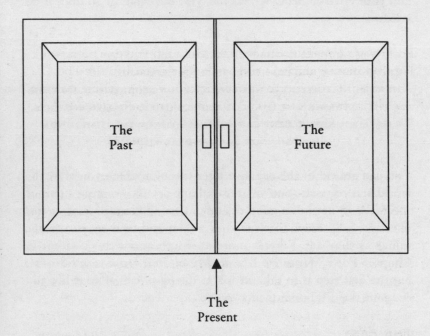

The Past

The Future

The
Present

As one of my teachers often said, *Stop trying to drive with your hands on the rear-view mirror!*

The first step is to realize that you can't change the past, only its effect on you.

WHEN YOU FIND YOURSELF DWELLING ON THE PAST IN A WAY THAT
MAKES YOU THINK LESS OF YOURSELF OR YOUR ABILITY TO MAKE
CHANGE, LET GO OF THE THOUGHT AND FOCUS ON WHAT'S
HAPPENING *RIGHT NOW*.

You really have only three possibilities when it comes to dealing positively with negative aspects of your past:

1. Forgive
2. Forget
3. Learn

Forgiving yourself is often the hardest. You've done your best. Forgive yourself and have compassion for yourself.

In order to forgive others, you need to have compassion for them as well. Can you understand and appreciate what it's like for them? Why did they do what they did? Did they get out of bed in the morning with the intention of hurting you or making life difficult for you? Probably not.

Some failures and disappointments we can just forget. As I look at my list each year, there are those which remind me of quite a long tale. So difficult and so painful, but so what? It's over and now it's just a story. Merely making the list and looking at it automatically releases much of the negative emotion associated with some of the things on it. And while we may not be able to forget our failures, at least we can ease their sting by neutralizing the effect of the negative emotion we've attached to them.

The best way to deal with the past is to learn from it, and that's the purpose of answering the third question, *'What Did I Learn?'* The principal value of our mistakes and our failures is to learn from them. As William Saroyan said, *'Good people are good because they've come to wisdom through failure.'*

LET GO

Again, the purpose of the first two questions in Best Year Yet is to re-balance our sense of ourselves and make room for new possibilities. Releasing our hold on the whip of resentment and regret is the first step. Most often these are the two underlying components of our disappointments and the dynamic that keeps them in place.

One of the ways to trigger your mind about the disappointments of the last year is to ask yourself, *What or whom do I resent?* Although you may find the answers come flooding into your mind, it's sometimes difficult at first to let ourselves write them down.

It's hard to admit to some of those feelings which at face value may look so petty and small. And difficult to let ourselves take a deep breath and face the pain they represent. But the opportunity of moving on from the pain and heartache caused by these feelings is worth all the discomfort of taking time to look them in the eye.

The anger, the sadness, the feelings of powerlessness and hopelessness drain us of our vital life energy. Once we start to neutralize these feelings, we're empowered to do something positive about the source of the problem.

WE HAVE THE ABILITY TO MOVE ON TO A HAPPIER STATE — LETTING GO OF RESENTMENT AND ITS COST TO US HAS BEEN PROVEN AGAIN AND AGAIN TO BE A FOOLPROOF PATH TO GREATER SUCCESS, HEALTH AND GENERAL WELL-BEING.

What good is the resentment doing you? Is holding on to the resentment making things better? What has been the result so far of holding on to that resentment? It's really so funny when I catch myself with a death grip on my resentment – *'I'm not going to let go until...*
they apologize.
they realize the error of their ways.
they finally listen to me.
they do things my way.
they stop driving me crazy!
etc., *ad nauseum.*
And in the meantime, I'm *not* going to let them off the hook. But who's miserable and who's stuck in the past? There's no possibility of growing anything different in a garden filled with this kind of poison.

So make some notes in response to the question about resentment and as you write your answers, think to yourself, *'Let go!'* Imagine pulling each weed as you go.

And then there are the regrets – things you wish you hadn't done and things you wish you had. Well, it's too late to do them *last* year but it's not too late for next year. You've got another chance. When thinking about last year, ask yourself *'What do I regret?'* Add your answers to your list for Question Two. Later you can come back to some of these and consider turning them into goals for next year.

But for now let them go. Remember their only real value now is their lessons. And in hindsight many of these experiences – both resentments and regrets – no matter how painful and difficult, are just what we needed at the time in order to grow and learn and move on.

OTHER'S EXPERIENCES

One of the advantages of doing this process with others or in a workshop is that you have the stimulation of their experience. In conversation, they let you know a bit about how they're answering these questions. To give you a chance to see how others have answered this question, two examples are on the following page.

The first is written by a young man – notice how his list is quite a mixture. Facts and feelings are combined as they occurred to him. It makes no difference – if it occurred to him, he wrote it down. Remember, whether something on your list is clearly one of your failures or a disappointment that isn't your fault but affects you deeply, write it down.

The second example is that of a woman – her list reveals that she's more neutral about some of the items on the list than others – it comes out in the way she's expressed herself – a perfect reflection of her mixture of disappointments for the last year of her life. The important thing is that she's taken the time to get it all down on paper.

WHAT WERE MY BIGGEST DISAPPOINTMENTS?

1. Gained a stone in weight.
2. My father died.
3. Ending relationship with Sue – still not over it.
4. Still earning the same as a year ago in spite of the fact that I deserved to get a pay rise.
5. Haven't taken any steps to find another job that I'd like better.
6. Trip to the US never materialized.
7. Joined the gym and only went seven times!
8. I didn't spend more time taking care of Mum – weeks go by and I forget to ring her.
9. Sex life is non-existent.
10. I never get a break – my health is beginning to suffer.
11. Feeling really ugly and stressed out.
12. Let my credit cards build up to over £2,000.

WHAT WERE MY BIGGEST DISAPPOINTMENTS?

1. Didn't meditate past the first month.
2. Feeling tired and drained – don't want to cook another dinner.
3. Bitter about how busy Peter is – always late, working at weekends. How will I ever get to know his children?
4. Want to get back to work, but have failed utterly to do anything about it – feel that I'm losing my nerve.
5. No time to myself.
6. Having the private weekend in Paris with Peter cancelled at the last minute.

WHAT DID I LEARN?

Men stumble over the truth from time to time
but most pick themselves up
as if nothing had happened.

SIR WINSTON CHURCHILL

LESSONS LEARNED

Look back over your answers to the first two Best Year Yet questions to see what you've learned. In reviewing what you accomplished, what possible lessons do you see?

> WHAT YOU'VE ACHIEVED SO FAR IS THE GREATEST SOURCE OF INFORMATION FOR YOU. THE SAME STRENGTHS, SKILLS AND QUALITIES YOU USED TO ACHIEVE THEM IS STILL AVAILABLE FOR NEXT YEAR.

Take a minute to make notes of your answers to questions such as:

- *What was the secret of my success?*
- *What worked?*
- *Why was I able to achieve what I did?*

Now take time to read over your answers to the second question –
your disappointments and failures.

- *What didn't work and why?*
- *What would have worked better?*
- *What's the lesson?*
- *Have I learned it yet?*
- *Is there evidence to prove that I've learned it? What is it?*

As you think back over your last year, there are lessons you've
learned and others you *could* learn, given what happened. First find
the ones you've really learned – there'll be evidence that you've
learned these lessons and have moved on. Don't be too hard on
yourself – if you *think* you've learned something, you have. It's
important to capture it now so you can remember it and avoid having to learn it all over again.

Then there are the potential lessons. If only you'd done it differently. If only you'd not done it at all. If only you'd done it in a
better way. What advice do you have for yourself? It's time to move
beyond guilt and recrimination – let yourself off the hook – assess
what you did and how you want to do it next time.

Answering Question Three gives you a big opportunity – to learn,
to change, to take on the challenges and to make the moves you've
been wanting to make. What would you have to do differently next
time in order to have a better chance of success? What would it take?

As you begin answering this third question, it's necessary to think
– to think more deeply about who you are and how you operate.
This kind of thinking is beyond the thoughts that just 'burp up'
spontaneously – really make your brain work; sweep away the fog
and find the answers. Trigger your mind with questions such as:

- *What changes do I need to make in the way I operate?*
- *How can I do things differently?*
- *What advice do I have for myself?*

- *Do I need more discipline?*
- *Have I been as honest with myself and others as I need to be?*
- *Am I taking care of myself as well as I need to?*
- *Do I face difficult problems as quickly as I should?*
- *Have I let others support me? Do I listen to their advice and seriously consider taking it?*
- *Am I as supportive of others as I want to be?*
- *What lessons are there for me in my work? Am I a salesperson who needs to be more proactive? a manager who needs to pay more attention to what others have to say? a leader who could provide more direction? or inspiration?*
- *Do I say 'thank you' often enough?*

WHEN WE TAKE THE TIME TO THINK, WE KNOW WHAT WE NEED TO DO AND WHAT WE NEED TO DO DIFFERENTLY. YOU *KNOW* YOUR MOST IMPORTANT LESSONS – WRITE THEM DOWN.

WHAT DIFFERENCE WOULD IT MAKE?

One of the greatest motivations to learn our lessons is to imagine the difference it would make to those around us if we did. In fact, sometimes our desire to help others can strengthen our resolve to change our behaviour.

But too often the lessons *others* need to learn are more obvious to us. Think about people you know and lessons you'd like them to learn. It's not difficult to see how much easier and more successful their life would be if only... The same is true for you.

So pretend you're somebody else and look at your life with a bit more distance. As you sit on the bank of your life's river, what do you see? What could you do to avoid more of the rocks and the boulders? What do you do that slows you down or stops you? Look at all the areas of your life: family, work, money, health, friends. What do you see? Look at other aspects: health, spirituality, service to community, doing your best at work.

Avoid judging yourself, you can move beyond that now. Practise thinking in new and more objective ways – keep imagining you are sitting in the corner of your own life watching yourself: What do you see? What do you like about what you see? What do you wish you'd do differently?

Rewrite the future – you know that if you change just a few ways of behaving, you can radically improve your chances of success. Think about just one of the lessons on your list. If you learned that one lesson in the next year, what difference would it make to you? Take the time to visualize yourself acting in this new way. Think about the potential benefits. *If I learned that...*

Once you've learned a lesson and are demonstrating it in your life, you've given yourself a gift like no other. Nothing can take it away from you. Not another person, not a major recession, not getting fired – nothing.

LIFE IS A CLASSROOM

The past year of your own life is a source of invaluable information. It tells you more about having what you want than all the lectures, books, videos and cassettes you can find. Your own experience of the past year is full of hints about success, increasing income, building positive relationships, gaining the kind of recognition you seek, achieving contentment and fulfilment and making the kind of difference you want to make. What does the information tell you about being the kind of person you want to be?

IN EXAMINING YOUR OWN LIFE, YOU FIND MORE GOOD SENSE THAN YOU CAN USE TO HELP YOU TO HAVE MORE OF WHAT YOU WANT IN YOUR LIFE.

Some of the lessons are so simple, it's embarrassing. Everyone knows them, we've heard about them from many sources – parents, teachers, preachers, bosses, friends, books... Even more embarrassing is the length of time we've waited to learn the lessons. When I think how many situations happened over and over again in the same way before I stopped making the same mistakes – instead of using good common sense I was following *these* 'rules':

- *Avoid opening the bills and reconciling the cheque book.*
- *Put up with relationships in which I'm made to feel small in order to feed someone else's ego because I'm too afraid to leave.*
- *Listen to other's troubles and don't ask for equal air-time.*
- *Work so hard that I don't have time to take care of myself.*
- *Do all the easy stuff and procrastinate about the action that would move me towards my goals.*

I could go on. Our lessons are all around us; if we want to have our Best Year Yet, year after year, we must wake up and see them. Becoming more aware of the gems in our own experience is better than striking gold. That only happens once, but our lessons pay off again and again.

As you begin to identify these lessons, the soil in your garden becomes enriched. You're starting to fertilize your ground and make way for growth. Thinking about mistakes and what you want to do differently starts to change the climate in which you live.

Consider how we learn about anything – for example, gardening. We get our information from a lot of sources – parents, neighbours, friends, gardening books. But the best source I've found are gardeners – people who are good at what they do and have demonstrated expertise over the years. When I'm in a tough situation or facing a big challenge, I sometimes think about someone (depending on the task at hand) and ask myself *How would he do this? How would she handle this challenge? What would he say now?*

Yet, at the end of the day, only when we go into action and learn our own lessons does the difference show up in our own lives. It's easiest to learn from ourselves. We know this information best. Some of our lessons we've been saying to ourselves many times over the years. *Why don't you…? What did you say that for? Wouldn't it have been better to…?* What annoys us most is when we hear friends giving us advice that's the same as we've been telling ourselves for years – but haven't heeded.

I've learned that I must use the information or continue to get the lecture – over and over again. My friend Lew Epstein often says, *'If only our ears could hear what our lips are saying,'* to refer to those times when we hear ourselves spouting wisdom that we'd do well to listen to ourselves. *Everything that irritates us about others can lead us to an understanding of ourselves,* said Carl Jung.

THE KNOWLEDGE IS THERE WITHIN US. WE HAVE ONLY TO THINK ABOUT THE ADVICE WE HAVE FOR OTHERS AND THEN HAVE THE HUMILITY TO SEE IF WE'RE FOLLOWING IT OURSELVES.

As you move forward answering this question, you're already changing your way of doing things. By consciously considering the lessons you have to learn, you've made your life into a classroom in which you can learn from your own mistakes and move on. Answering this question alone will make a difference in your next year.

TURNING YOUR LESSONS INTO PERSONAL GUIDELINES

If you haven't started your list, do it now. Write down all the lessons you can think of. Before you go on to the next step, make sure your list is complete and contains most of what you've thought as you've read through this chapter.

Now review the list. Think about each lesson and the difference it could make to you. Consider the changes you know you want to make now. Which ones could contribute the *most* to your success in making these things happen?

The next step is to choose your top three – the ones which, if followed in the next year of your life, could make the most difference to you and to those around you. Give this some time and choose the ones which are best for you right now. You may be drawn to them instinctively, taking very little time. If so, trust your intuition and go with it.

I'm not suggesting that you forget the rest of the lessons on the list, but I hope you'll have a few good years after the next one to work on them. One of the key things I've learned from working with people is focus, focus, focus. When you've finished your Best Year Yet process and you're back in the stream again, there will be only so much you can remember from this experience. Make it easy for yourself and give yourself every chance to win. Choose just three lessons for next year.

Once you've selected your three, turn them into instructions to follow over the next year. Take time to get the words just right. Each one should be as short as possible and stated as clearly and powerfully as you can. Start with verbs and make them punchy. Tell yourself what _to do_ rather than what _not to do_ – in other words, express them as positively as you can. It's difficult for you to know what _to_ do when the instruction is _not_ to do something. However, if you feel the lesson must start with a word like _Don't_ or _Stop_ in order for you to remember it, state it that way.

These three lessons are your Personal Guidelines for the next year of your life. You've already made a big step towards enriching the soil in which you'll plant your goals for next year. Take a quick minute to imagine how different next year could be for you by following these lessons

EXPERIENCES

One of my Personal Guidelines I call FACE THE MUSIC. By this I mean confront troublesome issues and relationships. Stop avoiding doing what needs to be done and pretending that everything's fine.

For years I would find myself in tough situations and difficult relationships and yet do nothing. Nothing except have angry internal conversations with myself and the other person – as I drove down the road or in the middle of the night or as I was making dinner – letting the bitterness build up and working myself to the boiling point. By the time something had to be done, it was too late to do it well. I was so filled with emotion and resentment – my side of the story – that I usually made a mess of it.

Gradually I'm learning to wake up and notice when something isn't right and then take action straight away. Book the time to think it through, come up with possible solutions, understand how the other person might think and feel and decide what to do and how to talk it over. Every time I succeed, the fog lifts and I'm again free and strong. And I've discovered that avoiding difficult issues is harder than dealing with them.

Another Guideline is USE A COACH TO SUPPORT ME TO DO WHAT I KNOW TO DO. I've been a professional coach to others for over fifteen years and too often I make the mistake of not having a mentor myself. It's a dangerous trap because I'm much more apt to do what I know works if I sit down and work with someone else, making a plan for myself, promising to carry it out and then meeting for a progress check in a month's time.

Over the past year I've begun using one again and it's made all the difference – the last year was definitely my best year ever and my coach was useful in keeping me on track as well as being a good listener during the rough patches when I needed to make important decisions.

One guideline I'm proud to say I've practised for years is DO THE TOUGH STUFF FIRST. You've most likely heard, as I have, that only 20 per cent of what there is to do really makes a difference, but knowing this and doing that 20 per cent are not the same. How easy it is to make a cup of tea, return non-urgent phone calls, chat with a friend or colleague and so on rather than tackle the one or two tasks that would make the most difference.

More and more often I just take myself to the top of the list and do that item first. My motivation is really a selfish one – as soon as that one is finished, I feel free and the rest of the day is easy. Sometimes it's a scary phone call or more often a report, a letter or a set of notes to write. Maybe the VAT return or reconciling the bank statement. Whatever it is and whether it takes five minutes or five hours, I've found it works to do it first. I'm not operating at 100 per cent on this, but I rarely let anyone down the way I used to do and I believe this is one of my cleverest guidelines for success.

Much of what I've learned about the value of identifying lessons has come from my work with clients. They've made the most progress through the process of taking responsibility for their own learning. They are their own best source of wisdom and advice – even though it's not always easy to follow.

When I'm consulting in a business I often work with teams of people who are working together to lead and manage the company. I start by carrying out an initial private interview with each executive to get his or her views on what's happening, how things are working and what issues need to be resolved. Almost without exception, they are quite clear – including stories and tales to illustrate – about where the problems lie and which people need to change. However, it seems I'm always talking to the innocent party. It's so easy to get out the 'blame gun' and point the trigger away from ourselves. However, when asked what they could do to resolve the issue, the conversation changes and most are willing to identify steps they could take to make positive change in the business.

The most powerful tool of a coach is asking questions. People have inspired me by their answers and by their willingness to own up to mistakes. When they get into trouble, it's rarely because of their doubt about what to do. They do know the answers and the lessons they need to learn. That's not the problem. The challenge is doing what they know how to do. Yet their courage is inspiring – how willing they are to see the problem, admit their part in it and think about what to do to make things work.

So in order to stimulate your thinking, the following are some examples of the Guidelines used by family, friends and clients:

- *Put my family first.*
- *Ask for help when I need it.*

- *Only stay in relationships in which I feel good about myself.*
- *Relax.*
- *Do what I know how to do.*
- *Face the music.*
- *Take the fun option.*
- *Take care of myself so I can take care of others.*
- *Do first things first.*
- *Be healthy.*
- *Let go, let God.*
- *Set aside time for myself and my husband.*
- *Enjoy the good in life.*

HOW DO I LIMIT MYSELF AND HOW CAN I STOP?

Life is a self-fulfilling prophecy.

HOW DO I LIMIT MYSELF?

Until I was 33 years old I didn't realize how much I was limiting myself. If you'd asked me this question before that time, I might have said, *Yeah, maybe a little...* but I hadn't begun to realize how much I limited myself or how I did it. I was much more aware of how situations and people around me were holding me back and how I had no choice, given my circumstances.

But I must have been limiting myself, because once I started to become more conscious about myself, things started to change. It was then that I got out of the back seat of my life (thanks to a great teacher and the support of many friends). Before then I rarely felt I was the source of my own experience or what happened to me – I was just a sleepy passenger in my life.

I was coping all right but felt generally frustrated, that something was missing. I was a disappointment to myself, lacking any awareness of how I came to be that way or what to do to make things different. At the rate I was going, I would never reach the place I'd hoped to go when I was younger, when I'd felt I had something to offer and could make a difference with my life.

I'd become an expert at explaining away situations and circumstances, living in silent sacrifice but for the most part not conscious of what I was doing. I was a good person – a mother with two small boys with a full life – but there were many unexpressed and unfulfilled longings. I'd come as far as I had only because I'd inherited a strong will and a good mind from both my parents.

When my journey of self-discovery began, I was shocked to find that my life up to then was just as *I* had created it. Instead of being a victim, I had shaped it by *my* thoughts and *my* actions. For instance, my relationships with my parents were a perfect reflection of my unexamined perceptions and attitudes about them. Until I woke up, my basic pursuit was to make sure *I don't grow up to be like my parents!* – an attitude that kept me from appreciating how much I'm like them and what a gift they are to me.

I now began to appreciate that if I had made my life the way it was so far, I had the tools to make it even better. But the first step was to discover how I had been limiting myself – and I invite you now to do the same.

IN ORDER TO HAVE YOUR BEST YEAR YET, YOU MUST DISCOVER HOW YOU LIMIT YOURSELF AND TAKE RESPONSIBILITY FOR WHAT'S HAPPENED SO FAR.

Of course, you're close to this way of thinking or you wouldn't be reading this book, but the habit of thinking of ourselves as victims rather than as the ones responsible is a strong one for most of us. A deep level of personal learning is available to you as you find out more about the context in which you're living your life and how it holds you back. In doing so, you discover the true meaning of Socrates' epigraph, *'The unexamined life is not worth living.'* The rewards of this particular process are beyond your imagination.

The following questions are designed to help you to discover your limiting beliefs and the behaviour that results. As before, ask yourself each question and let your inner voice respond. The answers are already there; you don't have to think to find them.

1. How do I limit myself?

....
....
....
....
....
....
....
....
....

As you begin to answer this question you may come up with all
kinds of reasons – write them all down. For example, here are some
answers given by others:

- *I don't take time to think about what's really important to me.*
- *I'm lazy.*
- *I believe what some other people say about me – their opinion
  carries more weight with me than my own.*
- *When I really fancy someone, I don't do anything about it.*
- *I don't stand up for myself.*
- *I don't follow through on what I say I'm going to do – I let myself
  down time after time.*
- *I never ask for a pay rise, just wait to see what they give me.*
- *I spend more than I make.*

2. What has it cost me to do so?

Although you're probably quite aware of this, take a minute to
confront the true cost of your answers to the question above – dig
to the bottom. Doing so begins to loosen the grip of your past and
how you think about yourself and what's possible.

....
....
....
....
....
....
....
....
....

Sample answers:

- *A lot of money.*
- *A feeling that I've not made the best of the gifts given me.*
- *Relationships with people who matter to me.*
- *A husband who respects me and whom I respect.*
- *Fulfilment and contentment.*
- *Self-respect.*
- *My health.*

You may notice that some of your answers to this question are reminiscent of the disappointments you listed in response to Question Two. This is fine – use this knowledge to reinforce your awareness of the connection between your thinking and your results.

3. In what ways have I benefited from limiting myself?

What, you say? How could *I* have benefited? The reason for asking this question is that we usually keep our limitations around because there's something in it for us. We're getting some reward from limiting ourselves and we're afraid we'd have to give it up in order to move on. At some level we know this and we hold on to our limitations so that we don't lose their perceived benefits.

It's especially important here just to ask yourself the question and write the answers that occur to you, whatever they are. Don't question your mental process – report your thoughts as you capture them and avoid the temptation to edit the answers as they pop into your awareness. The true meaning of your thoughts will become more clear after you think about what you've written.

Sample answers:

- *An easy life.*
- *Not having much expected of me so I don't have to work so hard.*
- *I can live in ignorance and not have to face up to all of it.*
- *Making sure people like me and approve of me.*
- *A husband (anyone) to blame it all on.*
- *I always have the handy excuse that I could do better if I really tried.*
- *Keep the peace – don't rock the boat!*
- *Self-respect.*

4. Am I willing to stop limiting myself?

The answer here is a simple yes or no. But it's obviously an important question. Don't worry about whether you think you're able or how you're going to go about it – just ask yourself *if I knew how, would I be willing to stop limiting myself?*

❑ Yes!   ❑ No.

If you haven't answered the four questions above,

STOP!

and go back and do so now. In order to connect fully with the important information that follows, it's important that you are fully involved in this process.

Once we're willing to become more aware of how we limit ourselves with our negative thoughts and beliefs, we're able to start seeing our past and its effect in a new light. One of the areas of greatest pain and unhappiness in my own life has been my relationships with men. When I started to dig into my attitudes and perceptions, I remembered an incident when I was a teenager. As you read on, notice how I limited myself by my thoughts alone!

A big school dance was announced, and this time the girls were to invite the boys rather than waiting to be asked. I'd fancied a football player named Mike for a long time and this was my chance. But it wasn't easy. Every morning I'd wake up convinced today was the day I was going to ask him, planning how to bump into him while going over and over what to say. But day after day I lost my nerve.

Finally, time was short and I had to do it. I walked over to him, looked up and said, *Would you like to go to the dance with me?* His answer? *No, I don't think so. Sorry.* What pain. I remember slinking down the school hallway, promising myself *I'll never let that happen to me again!* Now that I knew I wasn't good enough to go out with Mike, I knew I wasn't good enough, full stop. *I'll stay in hiding and see if anyone finds me. But I'm never going to get caught letting someone know I care. No one's going to make the mistake of thinking I presume to be good enough to have one of the good ones.* I now knew my place.

From that point onward, I lived in the past, dragging Mike along with me. Every time I met a new man, he met me – and Mike. Although I was hopeful, I still thought of myself as reject material. The more I liked a man, the more uncomfortable I was and the more I stayed in hiding, scripting every remark and every move. Mike took centre-stage and I stayed in the wings. I limited myself because of one two-minute experience and the decisions I made about myself as a result. My relationships with men were shaped by my firm perception that *I'd be lucky to have anyone, let alone one I really want.*

It wasn't until I examined this way of thinking – the context for my relationships with men – that I could see its hold over me and what it cost me over the years. Over and over again I settled for less than I wanted. In a period of self-examination such as the one shaped by Question Four, I shifted to a new way of thinking expressed by the statement *I can have any man I want!*

No sooner had I written this for the first time than I screamed at myself, *How unrealistic! Who am I kidding? What a laugh. Get serious!* – a typical reaction when we start to shift our fundamental limiting beliefs about ourselves. All our thoughts argue for our limitations. Our small mind is threatened. But I began to think in a new light about shifting the way I thought about myself and men. I took this seriously and began to see the possibility that *I can have any man I want* was more authentic than *I'd be lucky to have anybody.*

Shifting from this limiting perception to an empowering one is the finest gift I'd ever given myself. Within several months of making this shift, I met my Tim and I'm now married to a man whom I respect and love deeply, a man who is way beyond anything I ever thought was possible for me. But before I examined my self-defeating notions about men, he would have been way too good for me and I'd never have considered he might be remotely interested in me.

This may sound like an extravagant claim. Of course, we may have met, fallen in love and been just as happy without this profound shift in my perception, but you'll never convince me!

WHAT YOU FOCUS ON IS WHAT YOU GET

I hope you're able to see that as long as I thought of myself as a rejected woman, I'd be disappointed in love. The results in our lives are a perfect match for our expectations. How often we get what we predict we'll get! But it works both ways – negatively and positively. That's the magic. Wherever you have a positive focus in your life, you're probably getting good results. However, for the purposes of this exercise we're considering the negative aspects because that's where you'll find the secrets to moving to the next level of your personal effectiveness and power.

What are you focusing on now? What grabs your attention? I don't mean your coffee cup or this page in the book but rather your inner thoughts and attitudes. The purpose of the fourth Best Year Yet question is to help you discover your fundamental limiting perceptions about yourself and your life – ways of thinking and feeling which stop you from achieving what's really possible.

THE FIRST STEP IS TO REALIZE THE CONNECTION BETWEEN YOUR LIMITING THOUGHTS AND THE AREAS OF YOUR LIFE IN WHICH YOUR RESULTS ARE DISAPPOINTING. ONLY THEN CAN YOU SHIFT TO A NEW WAY OF THINKING THAT EMPOWERS YOU TO HAVE THE RESULTS YOU WANT.

But first look at the examples on the following page, culled from many people who thought about the connection between their inner focus and the results they were achieving.

What do I focus on?	What do I get?
My wide hips.	No dates.
Fear of failure in business.	Cash-flow crises.
Anger at not being treated fairly.	Not being treated fairly.
Resentment with my husband's preoccupation with business.	He pays little attention to me.
How little time I have.	Not enough time – behind in everything – out of control.

What are you thinking and worrying about? What are you *really* predicting for yourself, success or failure? Are you focusing on your fears or your strengths? Your doubts or your goals? Think about it – check out the premise that *what you focus on is what you get*. What's true for you? Don't believe a word I say unless it matches your experience.

Ask yourself, *what am I focusing on now?* Make a list of these thoughts and feelings down the left side of a piece of paper. Stop and do that now.

Then begin to think about what you're getting as a result of the focus of your thoughts and feelings. Look at the answers on the left and think about what's happening in your life. Is it possible that your relationships are a mirror of what you predict and expect? Is your career a reflection of your predictions? Ever catch yourself saying to yourself, *See!* or *I'm not surprised!* But this pursuit to be right rarely brings us the results we seek.

How are your thoughts and feelings related to what you're getting? Is there a link between your mental and emotional focus and what you're achieving in your life? Where do your thoughts and feelings lead you? Beside each item you've listed, write the actual results you have in this area of your life.

WHEN WE TAKE RESPONSIBILITY FOR OUR CAPACITY FOR POSITIVE
CHANGE, WE CAN CONTROL AND GUIDE OUR INTELLIGENCE AND OUR
FEELINGS AND POINT THEM TOWARDS THE RESULTS WE WANT. AS
THIS HAPPENS, WE ARE DRAWN TOWARDS OUR GOALS AS IF BY A
MAGNET.

When I took my focus away from my teenage rejection and focused
on what I wanted – *a lifelong relationship with a man I love and
respect* – that's what I attracted into my life.

The purpose of this line of questioning is to discover what's running your life – you or your limitations. Until you're aware of where
you are now, you can't change direction.

THE FRIED EGG

The model opposite is now called the Fried Egg, thanks to a client
who said that's what it looked like to him. It's actually a cross-sec-
tion of our mental and emotional makeup – a psychological model
to enable us to understand ourselves a bit better. It may at first be
difficult to grasp because it not only relates to our basic relationship
with ourselves but also begins to describe how the mind works, but
stay with it as this information is *the bottom line for making per-
manent lasting change*.

At the centre of each of us – the circle in the middle of the
diagram – is an experience of ourselves and our values; for most of
us what we call our heart or soul: WHO I AM. The part that never
changes.

Over time, more and more of this central core of inner strength
can become hidden beneath a layer of fear, anxiety, doubt and years
of habitual behaviour which no longer represents who we are. Our
failures are pointed out to us by well-meaning parents and teachers
in a way that focuses on the middle ring more than the centre – others speak to us in a way that makes us feel that there is something
wrong with *us* rather than with our behaviour or performance. We
then become WHO I'M AFRAID I AM and forget who we are.

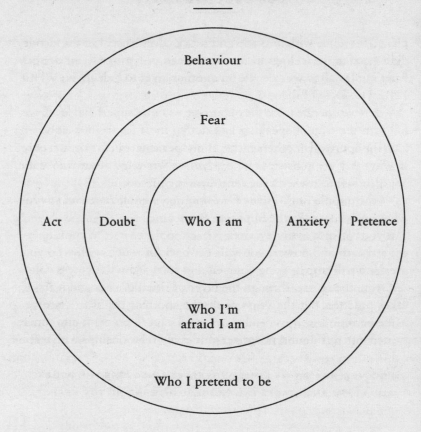

The resulting doubt and fear leads us away from behaviours which are consistent with our most deeply held beliefs and values. We begin to live as if the middle ring is the truth – as if the fear and anxiety are well founded; and then our feeling of worth is eroded. The middle ring of the diagram is the home of our limitations – the space within us where we store memories of self-doubt and fear. Once Mike said *No*, I began to identify with the layer of fear rather than my true self.

But most of us are too clever to walk around demonstrating our fears – I didn't lurk in corners acting the part of the shy reject! I played the game with bravado and mock confidence, but the façade didn't match the feelings inside. So instead of letting all our doubts hang out for all to see, we pile on another layer to hide them: WHO I PRETEND TO BE.

When we operate from the outer ring or more superficial level, we fall into the trap of speaking and acting in order to look good or gain the approval of others rather than speaking and acting honestly in ways that are consistent with what we want and what we value. We also lose touch with the centre and begin to think that the 'real us' is the middle ring. *Thank God they don't know how bad I am!* – what one client calls the Impostor Syndrome.

If you can move your awareness back to the centre, to your inherent strength and power, you will get back in touch with who you are. You will stop limiting yourself and start again to express yourself from the centre, through the layer of ritual doubts and fears. It takes practice, but the years of doubt and fear begin to dissolve. Mike became a memory and my painful experience with him (once turned into self-doubt) no longer guides my relationships with men.

DISCOVERING HOW WE LIMIT OURSELVES UNCOVERS THE DOUBTS AND FEARS AND STARTS THE PROCESS OF ERASING THE EFFECT THEY HAVE ON US.

HOW CAN I STOP?

So, how do we move beyond our self-defeating behaviours and shift our ways of thinking and feeling about ourselves so we stay in touch with our strength and value? Before you discover *what* you want in the next year of your life, take time to create the mental and emotional environment in which you can succeed.

A transformation occurs when you place yourself at the centre of your life, creating your world rather than letting circumstances dictate your success. You use your intelligence and your power to create a new reality for yourself. The process is one of shifting from a limiting to an empowering perception of yourself and the world in which you live. You shift from a false reality to an authentic one.

We're now ready to talk about the most powerful of tools for personal transformation: the Paradigm Shift. A paradigm is a way of seeing and thinking about yourself, someone else, an aspect of your life – anything. Think of a paradigm as a set of spectacles through which you see everything around you, including yourself. Except that you're not aware that the spectacles are there – you think you're seeing things as they 'really' are.

Once I was turned down for the dance, I established a paradigm for my relationships with men: *I'd be lucky to have anyone, let alone someone I really want.*

From that moment I lived inside that assumption – that was my reality, the truth for me. I was not aware of any other way of acting or thinking about the subject of men even though there was evidence that men were attracted to me.

OUR LIMITING PARADIGMS ARE NOT CORRECTED BY THE FACTS. WE KNOW WE'RE RIGHT AND NO EXTERNAL DATA CAN CHANGE OUR MINDS.

I've known hundreds of successful people whose personal paradigm was still limiting – no level of achievement, wealth or recognition would shift their perception of themselves. Once a limiting paradigm is in place, we must use our intelligence and our hearts to shift to a more empowering one. If we do not think of ourselves as successful or worthy, no achievement or level of recognition will shift this for us. It is an inside-out job!

Can you remember thinking that as soon as you earned £XXX, your troubles would be over? Were they? Have you ever told yourself that if only you could live with someone, you'd be happy? Was it enough?

CIRCUMSTANCES DON'T CREATE OUR REALITY, OUR HAPPINESS, OUR CONTENTMENT OR OUR FULFILLMENT. THAT'S *OUR* JOB.

When we make this fundamental shift in perception, we are able to stop looking at the future with eyes of fear. 'As a man thinketh in his heart, so he becomes' says the Bible. Learn to think about your strengths and your value.

You are the result of your thoughts and feelings. To change the results, change the way you think. Instead of investing your intelligence and energy in beliefs with negative outcomes, switch your focus to beliefs which lead where you want to go.

We each have many limiting paradigms, a sophisticated set of thoughts, excuses, defences – our reasons for failing. We put them in charge and we follow their lead – until we wake up. And when we do, the choice between reasons and results is clear. In Deepak Chopra's book *Ageless Body, Timeless Mind* he describes the paradigm of aging, a way of thinking that leads to degeneration and decay. He lets us know that we human beings have the intelligence and the capacity to shift to a paradigm of agelessness:

> There is no biochemistry outside awareness; every cell in your body is totally aware of how you think and feel about yourself. Once you accept that fact, the whole illusion of being victimized by a mindless, randomly degenerating body falls away.

The first step in your transformation is to discover your limiting paradigms. How do you think in ways that hold you back? What ritual doubts and fears shape your self-image? Answer the following questions to find your limiting beliefs.

1. In what areas of my life am I not achieving what I want?

....

....

....

....

....

....

....

....

Answer this first question quickly – just a list of points such as:

- relationships with women/men
- balance between work and play
- earning income
- creativity
- keeping fit

Now consider these aspects of your life and how you think and talk about yourself as a result of these failures. What do you say about yourself to explain these circumstances? What do you say to yourself about yourself? What do you say about yourself to others? In the answers you'll start to discover your own limiting paradigms.

2. What do I say about myself to explain these failures?

....

....

....

....

Your answers might sound like some of these:

- *No matter how hard I try, I'll never make it.*
- *I haven't got what it takes.*
- *Because I didn't go to university, I'm not clever enough.*
- *I'm too old – it's too late.*
- *I'm too busy – too much to do already!*
- *I don't deserve it.*
- *I'm lucky to have what I have now.*
- *I've got no choice.*
- *I'm probably earning more than I deserve now – hope I'm not found out!*

Remembering the Fried Egg model, think of your answers as the inhabitants of your middle ring. With these limiting paradigms in charge, where will they lead you? What you focus on is what you get, and paradigms create our fundamental focus in life. They dictate the size of our success, the quality of our relationships and the depth of our fulfilment. With these paradigms in charge, the results will be disappointing. Becoming more aware of them by writing them down begins to loosen their grip and starts to lessen their power over you.

We unknowingly empower these assumptions with our intelligence and then get results which are consistent with these limiting beliefs.

Once you feel your list is complete, at least for now, circle the ones that have the strongest influence on you. Which ones do you consider to be the truth? Which ones do you *really* buy into? Work with one of these as we move on to the technology of shifting paradigms.

PARADIGM SHIFTS

Finding your limiting paradigms is a giant step in awareness.

For much of my life, money was a problem. No matter what I did, I spent more than I earned and was always getting into trouble. Bills and bank statements hid in the desk drawers unopened and often it took threat of legal action to push me into a late-night panic of self-recrimination and scurrying to get my act together, yet again.

A couple of times I took out a credit consolidation loan from the bank, paid off my credit cards and my bills and wiped the slate clean. But I couldn't resist the temptation of spending up to the credit card limits again. I can't remember how many times this happened, but too many.

Nothing I did seemed to end the hopeless cycle because my actions were driven by a hidden limiting paradigm: *I want more money but I'll never make more than I'm making now – it's all I'm worth!* As long as I thought in this way, the results were the same, no matter what I tried to do differently. I was pulled by an invisible magnet back into the same pit.

But once I started to examine the limited ways I was thinking and feeling about money, the underlying paradigm became obvious to me. At a young age, I'd made a bunch of rules and decisions about money but they'd hid behind the cobwebs of my consciousness and I didn't know they were there. The results in my life should have given me a clue, but I didn't know how to discover their true meaning. Once I started to examine the way I thought about money, I found I'd created two fundamental rules which shaped my limiting paradigm about money and dictated the financial results I achieved:

1. *It's not all right to make more money than the man you're with,*
2. *It's not fair to make a lot of money when people are starving.*

Then there were the usual ones which nevertheless had a strong influence on me:

- *Money is the root of all evil.*
- *I'm not the kind of person to make a lot of money.*
- *Money is scarce – there's only so much to go around.*
- *If I made a lot of money, I'd be horrible and greedy.*
- *I don't have as much talent as people who make a lot of money.*

When I looked at my list to see which paradigm was the most influential for me, it was the one about people starving. I'd been convinced for so long that playing the money game would be a sell-out of my soul. How could I think about such a change? It was sinful to be so selfish.

But as I followed the thought, I realized that this paradigm of scarcity and unworthiness kept *me* poor as well as others. *What could my poverty contribute to them? What could I do for them when I couldn't even pay my own bills?* It was then that I realized that transforming my relationship with money was really a transformation in self-worth. I imagined that if I could get to the bottom of this one and start earning the kind of money I really wanted and secretly thought I deserved, I'd be in a stronger position – both within myself and within my wallet – to give to others. I wrote a new empowering paradigm for money in my life:

> *Money is abundant and flows spontaneously in life. Money allows me to express myself fully and contribute generously.*

This has been a source of inspiration and power to me over the past fourteen years. I now give more to others each year than my total annual earnings back then. My income now is many times what it was then. And it started by answering Question Four.

A New Empowering Paradigm for a New Year

Four Steps to Shift a Paradigm

1. Discover your limiting paradigm.
2. Think about what's holding it in place – limiting thoughts, feelings and perceived benefits.
3. Create a new empowering paradigm.
4. Learn the art of transformation: shift to your new paradigm whenever you become ensnared by your old, limiting one.

We've been through the first two steps of shifting paradigms. If you haven't already done so, choose the limiting paradigm you're going to shift in order to generate your Best Year Yet.

YOU DON'T NEED TO CHANGE EVERYTHING AT ONCE – START BY DISCOVERING *ONE* OF YOUR STRONGEST LIMITING PARADIGMS.

Now that you've completed the first two steps of shifting a paradigm, you can go to work creating a new way of perceiving and thinking that leads you to the results and relationships you want for yourself in the next year of your life.

Transformation is a fundamental change in the way you relate to who you are, what you do and what you have in your life. When you create a shift in paradigm, you take charge of your life.

Whether limiting or empowering, the dynamic of paradigms is the same. Each is represented by a statement which encapsulates our perception and what we believe. We think the statement is right and we use all our resources to create that reality – and it works. We prove the truth of that perception over and over again – in our thinking, feelings, actions, behaviour, results, relationships – everywhere. So you already have the ability to give truth to a paradigm – just shift to one which gives you a better return on your investment.

ONCE YOU UNDERSTAND AND ACCEPT THE DYNAMIC OF THE
SELF-FULFILLING PARADIGM, YOU CAN USE IT TO YOUR ADVANTAGE.

To write a new paradigm, look at your current, limiting one. What statement would describe a new perception that could destroy the old one? As you look at the following examples of limiting and empowering paradigms, you may feel that the empowering paradigms are 'too' positive or simplistic. Move past that thought. Instead, think about your limiting paradigm and what you'd rather make happen.

Limiting Paradigm	Empowering Paradigm
I'm lucky to have anybody.	I can have anyone I want.
I know best.	I enjoy learning from others and succeed far more quickly with their support.
I'm fat, ugly and hopeless.	I'm lean, strong and healthy.
I want more money but I'm not worth any more than I'm making now.	Money is abundant and flows spontaneously in my life.
I can't do what I really want to do.	I empower myself to have what I want.
I'm not good enough.	I have much to offer and I enjoy finding places to give.

Don't put limits on what you want to create for yourself. Decide what you want and write a statement that expresses it clearly. How do you do that? You make it up!

Your statement should express precisely what you want for yourself. When you first write it down it may exist only on the intellectual level. You'll have yet to experience its truth and you probably won't own it mentally or emotionally. But if it's a stretch for you to think in the way your new paradigm suggests, you're on the right track.

Notice the way in which the new paradigms above are worded. Each meets the following criteria for an empowering paradigm:

- Personal
- Present tense
- Positive
- Powerfully stated
- Pointing to an exciting new possibility

Once you have written your statement, make sure it's exactly right for you. Where does your new paradigm lead you? Exactly what results will you have when it comes true? Make sure the words express *precisely* the new reality you want to create.

REMEMBER, OUR PARADIGMS CREATE OUR RESULTS AND OUR RELATIONSHIPS.

Go beyond reasonableness and ordinary rationale. Make a quantum leap in your thinking. Allow yourself to think seriously about new possibilities and become enthusiastic about what could happen in your life. Expect a few miracles. Now that you have a new paradigm, you've given your garden its best dose of fertilizer. Imagine what's going to happen to goals planted in soil nourished by this paradigm. Albert Einstein thought that *imagination is more important than knowledge.*

IT'S TIME TO STAND APART FROM YOUR LIMITING THOUGHTS AND FEELINGS AND REPLACE THEM WITH ONES WHICH LEAD YOU IN THE DIRECTION YOU WANT TO GO.

Remember, this is the _truth_ about you, not positive thinking. As you read it, remind yourself *This is a statement about Who I Am.* Your limiting paradigm is a reflection of the middle ring – the doubts and fears. A lie. This is a statement of truth about you. You are moving on from the limited historical view of yourself and getting back in touch with your true self. Make sure that your new paradigm empowers you to achieve the goals you want for yourself in your best year yet.

When we are the victim of a limiting paradigm, we live an un-examined, unconscious life. If we stopped to think, we could see that our jumbled view of things was getting us nowhere. Many times our limiting paradigm is a paradox – so that are our internal messages are not only negative, they are conflicting. Look at the cartoon below. The thoughts on the right side of the head are pulling in the direction of having _more_ money. The thoughts on the left side argue for having _less_. As we know from physics, when two forces are pulling in equal and opposite directions, there is inertia. WE'RE NOT GOING ANYWHERE. Sound familiar?

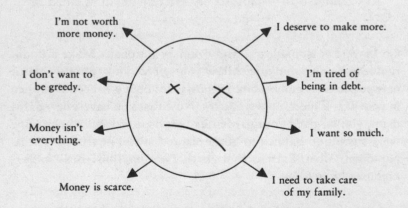

However, once we have an empowering paradigm – a focus we have consciously constructed to bring us what we want – we have one focus towards which to direct our intention and awareness.

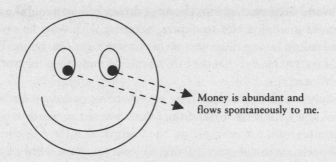

Money is abundant and flows spontaneously to me.

All our intellect and emotions are pointed in the same direction. In the cartoon above there's no dilution of energy or confusion of focus. While the person in the first picture seems at best to be headed round and round the roundabout, the second person is in the driving seat and knows where he or she is going. When you operate in this way, there is the possibility of a new reality based on personal truth, and you have a strong motivation to keep your eye on the road which leads you where you want to go.

How Do We Remember?

It's not always easy to keep this focus once we're out there on the road to our best year yet and life gets busy again.

Learn to catch yourself when your thoughts, feelings, attitudes and points of view are leading you back into your old perceptions. Stand apart from your thoughts and feelings and be aware of where they're leading. If they're going in the wrong direction, refocus on your new empowering paradigm. Say the words to yourself. Consciously shift the way you direct your intelligence and the investment of your emotions and intentions.

One of my most effective mental tricks is to envision my head as a bird cage. On one side of my head is the entrance, on the other the exit. I see my thoughts as birds who enter the bird cage. If they are limiting thoughts which don't lead where I want to go, I make sure the exit is open and imagine these 'limiting birds' flying right out again and disappearing into the air. I do my best to avoid the temptation of inviting a bird to dinner, agreeing with what he says and thus feeding him until he gets so fat he can't get out again. Then I could start to believe that the bird's limiting message is the truth and I'm hooked.

Many people write their new empowering paradigm on bits of paper and stick them around the house where the words will grab their attention, for example on the bathroom mirror or the front of the refrigerator. I once learned to look up every word of a new personal paradigm in the dictionary to give me a new level of understanding of and appreciation for its underlying intention.

BE CREATIVE IN YOUR PARADIGMS. DIRECT YOUR LIFE FORCE AND YOUR AWARENESS TOWARDS THE PERCEPTION THAT IS MOST ACCURATE AND EMPOWERING FOR YOU.

Above all, be aware of how you speak about yourself to others. While I'm not suggesting that you indulge in parrot-like iterations of your new paradigm at every opportunity, speak in ways that support your new sense of self. For instance, while I didn't talk with people about my new money paradigm, I did let people know at appropriate moments that money was no longer a problem for me.

To have your Best Year Yet, you must not only change what you do but you how think and feel. Changing either your external behaviour or your mental and emotional environment alone is not enough. Positive, lasting change comes from moving both at once.

Learning the science and art of the paradigm shift is life's greatest gift. Learning to design and implement your new paradigm is the secret to taking charge of your own life rather than being guided by the invisible hand of a limiting paradigm. What could be better?

_____

WHAT ARE MY PERSONAL VALUES?

It is not enough to possess virtue as if it were an art;
it should be practised.

MARCUS TULLIUS CICERO

WHAT'S DRIVING YOU?

The promise of this book is to put you back in the driving seat of your life. Becoming more aware of your personal values helps you to understand what really motivates you. Why, for example, do you pick up books like this? What are you looking for and why?

What drives most of us is the ambition to improve the quality of our lives while being true to ourselves and what's really important to us. Although we may not be conscious of these basic motivations as we live day to day, these hidden drives are the strongest in our lives. The more conscious we are of them, the more we empower ourselves to make the necessary changes in our lives.

When you examine the underlying drive for each of your conscious goals, you'll find out what really gets you out of bed in the morning. The more aware you are of this dynamic, the more genuinely enthusiastic you'll be to throw the covers off and get going.

When I ask people about what they want, they usually respond by saying something like a promotion, a new car, a holiday, more income, a husband or wife, a child. But usually there's something lying behind these goals – a less obvious goal or objective.

We may think, for example, that we want a new car, but is it the *thing* itself or what it represents to us? Is it the way we'll feel when we drive the car – the experience of pleasure or ease in getting where we want to go? Or is it how others will think of us when they see us with the new car – the feeling of prestige or wealth? Or perhaps, with some cars, it's a sense of power we're really after. Once we uncover the real goal, we can focus on it as well as the original more tangible goal and therefore have a better chance of getting what we truly want.

Perhaps one of your goals is to become more fit. Are you motivated by the moment you'll get your gold star from the doctor, or are you really pursuing greater energy or improved self-esteem? These intangibles are based on the personal value of *Taking Care of Yourself*.

The fact that we're unaware of these hidden unconscious 'drivers' is the reason we often don't feel satisfied when we finally achieve a goal. Ever had the experience of working as hard as you can for a long time to achieve a goal, only to feel let down when you finally reach it? Often it's not the achievement itself we're after but the experience we're hoping it will provide us with when we do achieve it.

When I discovered that it wasn't 'more money' itself I was after but the chance to express myself fully and contribute more generously, I had a major breakthrough in my ability to generate money. I connected the goal with two strong personal values: *Self-Expression* and *Contributing to Others*. For example, if you have a family your desire for more money is possibly not the money itself but the chance to be true to your personal value of *Loving My Family*.

If your objective is to get a promotion at work, more money may be your tangible objective but the desire for a greater sense of achievement and more recognition of who you are and what you're capable of could be your underlying and more intangible aims. The personal value of *Expressing Myself* or *Self-Actualization* are more likely what keeps you going.

Underlying most of our tangible goals, like a home, car, money, holidays or clothes are the intangible goals which bring us to a greater manifestation of our personal values. When we are aware of these values, we see a clearer picture of who we are and, more importantly, find the greater motivation to make change in our lives.

BASIC LIFE PURSUITS

One of the biggest blocks on the road to full self-expression is the underlying assumption that we're *still* not good enough to be the kind of person we'd really like to be! This feeling springs from the limiting paradigm – *What can I do to prove myself? To be good enough?* Our life pursuit of changing ourselves is often built on the lie that we're not good enough already and need to do something more before we can truly show what we are.

And where does this self-limiting paradigm lead us? We waste vast amounts of energy striving to prove ourselves, our worth and our value. We look for approval more than results. And it's easy to fall into the trap of valuing others' opinions more than our own.

Years ago I got a good roasting from a colleague, who accused me of being totally self-serving in my approach to my work. It took me months of soul-searching to come to my senses and realize that what she said was inaccurate and that her assumptions were incorrect. I understood why she attacked me but I knew her perception was not true. During this very painful process I strengthened my commitment to live according to my personal values and to trust my motivation to contribute to others.

I've seen board executives in large companies who think and act as if they were still waiting to be given permission to take the ball and run with it. Instead of making the changes they've been longing to make once they rose to a position of leadership and influence, they still hold back, afraid to take the lead they've earned.

Use the model below to consider your own life pursuit. Is it characterized by the circle on the left or the one on the right? How are you investing your intelligence and your life-force? If you see that you're engaged in Life Pursuit I, your awareness and your commitment to shift to Life Pursuit II are sufficient to make a fundamental difference in your life.

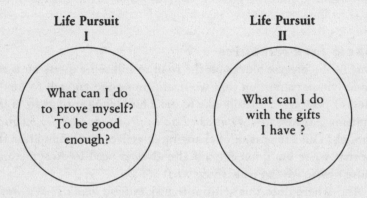

Life Pursuit I

What can I do to prove myself? To be good enough?

Life Pursuit II

What can I do with the gifts I have ?

Sometimes it takes a bit of time to figure out what we're doing and which pursuit we're engaged in. When Tim and I were first married, we would sit at the dinner table in the evenings having our meal, sharing a bottle of wine and talking over how the day went. He was starting a company and found himself in a position of leadership and total corporate responsibility for the first time in his life. Although it was what he'd always wanted, it was frightening and scary now that the time had come to make it happen.

Every time he faced another new challenge – making his first cash flow, getting in more sales, training new staff – he'd have another attack of self-doubt. He was open with me and let me know how he was feeling. Night after night I reassured him, reminding him of his strengths. After months I noticed a familiarity about our conversations – they didn't seem to be making him feel any better. I realized

I'd become part of the problem and was feeding into his paradigm of Life Pursuit I. We had to stop playing this game in order to help him to empower himself. One night when he was sharing his doubts about himself, I said *You know, maybe you're right. You might not have what it takes!* That was the end of that game.

This lifelong habit of insufficiency and unworthiness can be transformed into the healthier and more fulfilling Life Pursuit II – *What can I do with the gifts I have?*

Life Pursuit II is based on an empowering paradigm – one which places living up to one's values ahead of ego and survival. It is driven by the values such as the desire to make things work, to support others, to make the best use of our gifts and to keep our promises. Living in the context of this pursuit makes all the difference to our approach to life. There's no time to indulge in self-doubt and fear – there's too much to do.

Life Pursuit I is focused on personality and superficial self-improvement. When we're captured by this game, we're self-absorbed, inwardly focused and, I believe, generally wasting our time trying to work out what's wrong with us. There are the breakthroughs and the realizations, but a person in this trap never changes his or her basic life story – there are new chapters perhaps but always within the same overall plot: I'M NOT GOOD ENOUGH.

One of my finest teachers worked hard to teach me this lesson. Once in a meeting he said to me, *You remind me of an orange tree straining to grow an orange*. It took me weeks to figure out what he meant, but eventually I realized he was telling me that I was caught up in Life Pursuit I and that this was a waste of my time and energy. An orange tree grows oranges it doesn't waste one molecule of energy worrying about whether it has what it takes to do so. Sounds ridiculous, doesn't it?

But that's exactly what we do when we waste time in self-doubt and fear rather than focusing ourselves on what we can do right now with what we have. Imagine starting your day with the intention of discovering where you can use your talents. What difference would that make to you in your life? When I have seen people rely on their strengths and get on with it, it is inspiring.

I spent most of the first year of my marriage being upset and demanding more love from Tim. *Why are you so tired all the time? Why don't you help out more around the house? Why don't you ever get home when you say you will? Why don't you initiate some of our social arrangements? Why don't you book the theatre, the cinema, our holidays...* and so on. In short, I was asking him, *Why don't you love me more?* This was Life Pursuit I at its epitome: I was trying to get Tim to prove he loved me, time after time so that I'd know *I* was good enough.

And then one day I woke up. Given that *I* wanted a loving relationship, I wasn't acting consistently with that value. In fact, I was doing just the opposite by creating an upsetting atmosphere of argument, complaint, justification and anxiety. I was the one who was creating it. He wasn't complaining. I was.

I realized that if I wanted a loving relationship, it was up to me to make it that way. I knew I had the power, that was the Good News: if I wanted it to be different, I had the power the change it. But then there was the Bad News: it wasn't a question of whether I was *able* to do it, it was whether I was *willing* to take the leading role in making our relationship a loving one. It was whether I was willing to stop withholding my love while waiting for him to change. It was whether I could give up the '*I will if you will*' game.

What enabled me to change the way I was acting was the realization that I was not behaving in a way that was consistent with my values, with what I believed in. I was acting like a victim. I was *reacting* to my environment. I was expecting my husband to provide me with the relationship I wanted. Once *I* began to be the way I wanted the *relationship* to be – in a word, loving – the relationship moved from strength to strength. I switched to Life Pursuit II in my marriage. I found that *marriage is an opportunity to love*, not a place to prove I'm OK or that *I'm* loved.

And guess what? Tim's been far more loving, supportive, romantic, helpful – all I wanted. But it was no accident. And it started with my being true to my value of loving.

Life Pursuit II is outwardly focused. It incorporates an awareness of our world and the people in it, a consciousness of the effect we have on people, problems and circumstances. But this does not mean self-sacrifice for the sake of others. The first responsibility of any person engaged in Life Pursuit II is to take care of him- or herself.

You're not on an assembly line, you're a finished product. Start the ignition and drive!

WHAT'S MOST IMPORTANT TO YOU?

What really gets you out of bed in the morning? Why do you work so hard? What drives you to do what you do? Your first automatic response may be that you have no choice – again, the victim of circumstances. But it's time to go beyond that level of awareness to find out what you're really up to.

Who are you and what values do you want to demonstrate in your life?

Find the drive in you that's so strong it could motivate you to generate a new kind of life for yourself. Take the time to discover the personal values which are forceful enough to drive you to live from the new empowering paradigm you've created for yourself.

When we do this, we tell ourselves *I've had enough! I'm good enough and I'm ready to get going.* With this kind of determination, you can break through the self-doubt and pretence of the Fried Egg model and express yourself more fully in your life. You can move past your laziness, inertia, failures, excuses and feeling of resignation, and move on to your Best Year Yet.

WHAT ARE YOUR PERSONAL VALUES?

Your values are your personal principles or standards – your judgment of what's important or valuable in your life. They are deeply held beliefs which live in the heart and soul of each of us. We want them to shape the way we work, make choices and take care of our loved ones. They form the very foundation of every human being.

As you define your personal values, beware of a potential limiting paradigm such as *I'm not a good person*. This just gives you another excuse to fail, thereby proving to yourself either that you're not living up to your values or, worse, you don't have admirable principles to begin with. Another manifestation of Life Pursuit I.

Awareness of our personal values and our commitment to Life Pursuit II averts our attention from hidden, destructive, negative drivers, such as:

- Resentment
- A need to get even
- A desire to generate sympathy in others
- The 'I'll show them' syndrome
- Martyrdom
- Wanting to make others sorry for the way they treat you.

One way of thinking about what's important in the grand scheme of things is to think about the end of your life. How do you want to be remembered? What do you want on your tombstone? What do you wish others to say about you as they stand around at your funeral? Above all, for what do you want to be admired?

When I've worked with people and led them through this enquiry, the same personal values surface over and over again. They are fundamental and undeniable and hold true for all people. Common on people's lists would be values such as:

- Integrity
- Taking care of myself
- Loving family
- Self-actualization
- Making a difference

- Keeping promises
- Honesty
- Trust
- Peace of mind
- Happiness
- Compassion for others
- Respect
- Sense of accomplishment
- Demonstrating my best
- Expressing myself

Think about your personal mission and values. Ask yourself such questions as:

- *What values represent who I am?*
- *What values do I want to demonstrate?*
- *What do I want to happen as a result of my interaction with others?*
- *What effect do I want to have on others?*

What Are My Personal Values?

Take time now to write down your own personal values.

....

....

....

....

....

....

....

....

....

....

The aim here is to clarify your values and strengthen your awareness of them in your heart and mind. Fundamental principles or values do not change. Whether you're demonstrating your belief in these values is another issue which you can address as you plan your next year – but don't doubt them.

IF YOU REMEMBER INSTANCES WHEN YOU WEREN'T TRUE TO YOUR VALUES, THINK OF THEM AS TIMES WHEN YOU WEREN'T BEING YOURSELF. WE ALL MAKE MISTAKES – BUT WE CAN LEARN FROM THEM AND MOVE ON. THAT'S LIFE. AS LONG AS YOUR ROOTS ARE STRONG, YOU CAN GROW AGAIN AND AGAIN. THAT'S THE WAY OF NATURE.

BEYOND THE GOODIES

Living a life based on personal values takes us to a place in which we are motivated by more than the acquisition of 'goodies' – our material world and its pleasures. There's nothing wrong with these, but they are milestones rather than the true reason for living. Don't get me wrong, I'm not an ascetic – far from it. But the purpose of my own goodies and the pleasure they bring is to nourish and replenish my spirit so I am better able to fulfil my mission in life. As an end in themselves, they don't provide satisfaction or fulfilment.

The decade of the 1980s has been called the age of greed – one in which so many got caught up in the 'goodies game' for its own sake. We know of many people who in the process failed to live according to their fundamental life principles, and who got caught red-handed. Part of the value of the Maxwells of this world is to wake us up to what happens to people caught in the act of not being true to others or themselves.

Becoming more aware of your personal values and raising your consciousness about them is an invaluable step towards your Best Year Yet. The process awakens your strongest drivers and your most natural motivations.

In truth, there's no hiding place for any of us. We're not invisible.

We see others fully and they see us in the same way. When we speak and live our personal values, it's obvious. When we forget, the same. But when we become more conscious of our personal values, we can make sure that the person the world sees is someone we are proud of.

As you go along, catch yourself being true to yourself; appreciate yourself – it's a great motivator! One of my client friends carries out what he calls his Pillow Check each night before he goes to sleep. He reviews what happened during the day, when he lived in a way he was proud of and when he could have done better.

Dare to be who you are. Break through the barrier of self-doubt and pretence to express your true self. Let yourself be seen more fully as you live more in line with your values. The first few steps as we come out of hiding can be frightening, but the sense of freedom and fulfilment that results is enormous.

WHAT ROLES DO I PLAY IN MY LIFE?

It often happens that I wake at night and begin to
think about a serious problem and decide I must tell the Pope about it.
Then I wake up completely and remember that I am the Pope.

POPE JOHN XXIII

WHY THINK ABOUT ROLES?

Answering this question allows you to get an overall view of all the aspects and responsibilities of your life.

Stopping to think about the various roles I play has always brought me back to sanity at times when I found myself chasing my tail and my TO DO list, wondering if I'm getting anywhere or just wearing myself out.

LOOKING AT YOUR LIFE FROM THE PERSPECTIVE OF THE ROLES YOU PLAY PROVIDES A SENSIBLE WAY OF INTEGRATING THE VARIOUS AREAS OF YOUR LIFE WHILE PLACING YOURSELF AND YOUR VALUES AT THE CENTRE, DIRECTING THE SHOW.

There are many additional benefits of thinking of your life from the vantage point of the roles you play; let's explore some now.

1. Provides direction

Whether I think of myself in my role as a mother or a coach, I can create a timeless sense of myself and see the river of my life, where it's going and where I'd like it to go. I picture myself in the centre, in control and able to guide myself in the direction I want to go while maintaining an awareness of my principles.

Thinking of your roles enables you to direct yourself and design your life with a meaning beyond that of just improving your lot. You create a continuum of values allowing you to strengthen your sense of self – the one who guides the playing of each role in your life. You move to a place beyond the illusion of thinking you have no choices.

2. Places WHO YOU ARE – your values – at the centre of your life

As you make a connection between your roles and how you play them, you're able to consider how you would play each role in line with what's most important to you. It is a far more valid and validating way of measuring success in life.

AWARENESS IS EVERYTHING. JUST THINKING ABOUT YOUR ROLES AND YOUR VALUES SHIFTS THE WAY YOU THINK ABOUT YOURSELF AND YOUR LIFE. IT PUTS YOU IN THE DRIVING SEAT AS NOTHING ELSE CAN.

I have often found personality-driven self-improvement dictums confusing simply because I couldn't figure out how to follow suggestions such as *Stand up for yourself* or *Be more assertive* without feeling that I'd be selling out in some way or walking all over the people around me. When you focus on your roles and values, however, doubts and fears dissolve. You will find, for example, that the true expression of the personal value of 'loving my family' makes it impossible *not* to assert yourself in your role as partner and parent.

3. Makes Life Pursuit II the natural option

As you think of your life from the viewpoint of the roles you play, you are naturally looking outward. It's difficult if not impossible to wallow in self-pity or indulge in self-doubt when your eyes and your awareness are focused outside yourself.

Think of a time when you've helped a friend in trouble. Did you spend time wondering if you were able to do it or did you just get on with it, giving it everything you had?

When you're conscious of your desire to play the role of friend and have a mental image of how you want that to look and be, it dissolves the need to prove yourself or waste your energy in needless approval-seeking. The spotlight is off yourself and on what you want to provide. The transformation of focus from personality to values happens and you're free. Ego disappears and thoughts of *How am I doing?* dissolve.

4. Generates balance in your life

One of the most common complaints I've heard from people over the years is that their life is out of balance. Too much time and attention is being spent on one or two areas of their lives and not enough on others. The cost is high.

Too many times in the course of my work I've met middle-aged workaholics who have turned around after 20 years of Type A behaviour to discover they're alone, and that it is almost impossible to rebuild the bridges that could easily have been kept in good order as the years went by – without, I believe, any cost to their business success. Quite the reverse.

Working from the perspective of roles ensures that nothing is left out of your life. One important aspect of the Best Year Yet process is a short weekly review session in which you think about your roles and what's most important to achieve in each of them for the coming week. In this way you provide checkpoints for yourself and move step by step towards the goals you have for the next year. Momentum builds and your personal strength and power grow as you become more and more true to yourself and what's important to you. (The full system is outlined in the chapter on Question Ten.)

This easy method helps you to make sure you don't disappear down a dark hole with a total focus on just one role or one project within one role of your life. While I obviously spend more time in some roles than others over the course of a week, I'm accomplishing something important in each role. I'm able to make valuable distinctions between intention and time. It takes a surprisingly short amount of time to make a strong connection, for example, with someone in my family.

Much of life's stress, anxiety and depression comes from being more narrow and limited in your life focus than you truly want to be. I have embarrassing memories of several times when I became so caught up with a new man I let everything else slip. And in the end I'd always lose both myself and the relationship.

5. Increases your natural motivation

When you're making what you think and feel are the right choices for you and you're seeing them through, your momentum and natural energy increase. This cycle becomes self-perpetuating and positive and you're naturally pushed to make the changes you want to make – not to get better but to become more effective in playing your roles.

WHEN WE'RE BEING TRUE TO OURSELVES AND DOING WHAT REALLY MATTERS TO US, WE ARE LIVING OUR LIVES WITH INTEGRITY.

One of the biggest lessons I have learned is that *Much suffering comes from a lack of integrity*. When you've integrated yourself from the perspective of your roles, you have the life design which supports you to live with integrity. Energy and enthusiasm return and it's no trouble to keep going – you can't stop yourself.

WHAT ARE YOUR ROLES?

As you define your roles, remember this is your list just for now. It's often necessary to drop old roles, add new ones or change some as circumstances change.

Think first about the roles you're currently playing:

- *What are my current responsibilities?*
- *What am I accountable for in my life?*
- *What do I do during the day? the weekends?*
- *What would I call the role I'm playing as I'm doing each of these activities?*

Consider the roles you're not actively focused on now but feel you should be doing more with. For instance, are your relationships with your parents what you want them to be? Maybe you haven't given attention to the role of Son or Daughter over the past several years, but now want that to change. In this case this role would then be on your current list of roles.

Give your imagination a chance, too. What roles are you not playing but would like to play? This year is the first time that Writer is on my list of roles, although when the year started and I did my Best Year Yet process, I hadn't yet written a word. Putting it on the list got me moving. How about Painter, Adventurer, Actor, Student, Salesperson, Sailor – what dream role do you have?

Here are titles of some examples of names others have given to the roles they play in their lives:

Parent	Lover
Son, daughter	Husband
Family member	Wife
Home-owner	Cook
Manager	Deacon
Receptionist	Homemaker
Fundraiser	Friend
Director	Poet
Salesman	Designer
My own minder	Adventurer

Above all, I believe one of your roles needs to focus on taking care of yourself – being your own Coach or Caretaker. However you want to name this role and in spite of being engaged in Life Pursuit II, you must take care of yourself so you can take care of others and carry out your responsibilities.

You are the one who plays these roles and needs the strength, stamina, health and inspiration to live according to your values. As you review your performance and your intentions for each role every week, you'll be able to think about what *you* want or what you need to do for yourself. A life shaped around Life Pursuit II does not ignore the self – quite the opposite. It's impossible to play other roles with any degree of effectiveness if we're worn out, stressed and resentful.

Once you've made your full list of roles, count them. How many are there on your list? If there are more than seven or eight, I strongly recommend that you consolidate several roles to narrow your focus. Just as managers must limit the number of their direct reports in order to stay sane and able to direct, coach and empower each person, you should limit your roles in order to win at self-management. Give up a sense of complication and avoid the feeling of being overwhelmed – set yourself up to win.

'OUR LIFE IS FRITTERED AWAY BY DETAIL. SIMPLIFY, SIMPLIFY' WAS THE ADVICE OF THE AMERICAN POET HENRY DAVID THOREAU.

This year my roles are:

1. Jinny's Coach
2. Writer
3. Coach
4. Wife
5. Mother
6. Family Member
7. Friend
8. Homemaker

For example, in order to simplify, everything to do with taking care of the home, car and money is included in my role as Homemaker. My relationships with my (and Tim's) parents, aunts, uncles, sisters, brothers, nieces and nephews are encapsulated in my role as Family Member.

Think about the roles you're currently playing, feel you should play more or want to add to your life. List them opposite, remembering to integrate roles so that you have no more than eight main roles to consider as you go forward in the Best Year Yet process.

My current roles:

1.
2.
3.
4.
5.
6.
7.
8.

LINKING ROLES AND PERSONAL VALUES

You now have two valuable pieces of information about yourself: your Personal Values and your Roles. In order to begin to integrate the two in your thinking, look at the matrix below.

Personal Values:

Roles:	Love	Honesty	Trust	Integrity	Doing my best	Compassion	Personal Responsibility	Empowerment
Personal Coach	✓	✓				✓	✓	
Manager			✓	✓	✓			✓
Salesman				✓	✓		✓	
Husband and father	✓	✓	✓		✓	✓		✓
Church Member	✓			✓	✓	✓		
Family Member	✓						✓	
Friend	✓	✓	✓			✓		
Home-owner				✓			✓	

Importance of Values in Each Role

This man has listed his roles down the left-hand side of the graph and his personal values across the top. He can now do several important bits of thinking in order to clarify how he wishes to demonstrate his personal values in different aspects of his life. In this example he has thought through each of his roles, asking himself, *Is this value of __major__ importance in this role?* Obviously there's space for each value in each role, but in order to begin to shape each specific role, he has chosen values which he felt were vital to his success in each role.

Personal Values:

Roles:

Importance of values in each role

Here is a form for you to use for your own thinking – or you can make a simple matrix of your own on a pad of paper.

In addition to going through the process of deciding which key values you want to demonstrate in each role, you can also carry out a quick self-assessment on the same form. How do you feel your current behaviour is reflected in each role? Use a different colour pen and tick the values you're currently demonstrating in specific roles. Go down the column for each value, ticking the roles where you feel you're demonstrating this value in the way you want to. In this way you know where your journey begins – you start with a positive focus.

AWARENESS INCREASES AND BRINGS ITS OWN REWARDS. WHEN YOU BEGIN TO CONNECT YOUR PERSONAL VALUES WITH YOUR ROLES, THE UNCERTAINTY LIFTS AND THE DESIRE TO LIVE LIFE PURSUIT II IS AN EASIER ONE.

You now can point yourself in an outward direction and become more proactive in the planning of your own life. A natural outcome is that you start to ask yourself such questions as:

- *How am I going to help my son?*
- *What can I do to ensure that I get the pay rise I need?*
- *When can I book some time with my husband?*
- *If I'm really going to write a book, what's the first step?*
- *What does my mother need from me?*

Consciousness increases and begins to shape your life in new and more empowering ways. I've found that living with a focus on roles and personal values has reduced stress and increased my sense of fulfilment. I now have a method for making sense of things and bringing myself back into balance on a regular basis.

I know it takes courage and determination to appreciate more deeply who you are and what you want in your life, but the experience is profound and worth every ounce of discipline it takes to make yourself do it. Your personal values and your intentions for each role take the lead in your life and give it shape and direction. Be selfish for a short time now so you can decide where you stand and what you stand for.

One of the principal benefits of directing our lives in this way is an increased sense of purpose, making it easier to answer tricky questions such as *Who am I?* and *What am I doing here?* or *What's the point?*

How Do You Intend to Play Each Role?

Although Best Year Yet is focused just on the next year of your life, you can start to envision a longer-term view of how you want to live each role. Once you can see a mental picture in your mind, you'll naturally be drawn to living in that way.

Take just ten minutes to look at your list of roles. Quickly focus on each role, one at a time, and see yourself acting in the role in the way that would most demonstrate what's important to you and that would match your values. As you go through each role, ask yourself *How will it look? feel? sound?*

Think about how you would like to be seen to be carrying out each of your roles. This is just preliminary thinking and planning, but in this way you start to plant the seeds which can grow into your greater effectiveness in each role. What are the outcomes you'd like as a result of playing each role? As you begin to direct yourself to live your roles with more awareness, what guidelines or advice do you have for yourself?

- *In my role as a wife, I want to do more appreciating and less complaining.*
- *As a husband, I'd like to listen more fully to my wife.*
- *When I talk to my son, I want to ask more questions and really listen to what he has to say.*
- *I want to be more honest and helpful with my friends, letting them know what I really feel.*
- *With each person in my family, I want to spend more time thanking and praising than dispensing my infinite wisdom.*
- *At the office I want to speak up and say what I think.*

As you answer Questions Seven and Eight of Best Year Yet, you'll begin to focus in on your goals for the next year of your life. Having seen the bigger picture in your mind's eye helps you identify what steps and what changes you want to instigate in the next year, knowing that each is on the way to the future you're creating.

Do remember your most important role – taking care of yourself. What do you want to do for yourself to help you to be able to fulfil these roles in the way you want? What advice do you have for yourself so that, for example, you can be loving, healthy, calm and happy as you play each role?

As you envision yourself in your roles, give major attention to succeeding in this most important one – looking after yourself. It's essential to take care of yourself in order to be stronger and more resilient – able to stand at the centre of your life rather than getting buffeted around by external forces.

WHICH ROLE IS MY MAJOR FOCUS FOR THE NEXT YEAR?

Never mention the worst. Drop it out of your consciousness.
This practice will bring all of your powers to focus on the attainment of
the best.
It will bring the best to you.

NORMAN VINCENT PEALE

WHOLE LIFE REVIEW

Before making your choice of which role will be your main one for
the next year, give yourself some altitude in your thinking – about
your life and the roles you play in it. Imagine you're in a helicopter
rising above your life, looking down at everything at once. See yourself scurrying around carrying out your roles and responsibilities.
Allow yourself to take a neutral view of what you do and who you
are – to assess the whole of your life before deciding where to focus
your efforts in the next year.

The purpose of this seventh step in the Best Year Yet process is
to create a breakthrough in your life by selecting one of your roles
as your major focus of attention. Other roles will have goals as well,
but there will be one area in which you'll want or need to make the
most improvement or biggest change right now.

As you look down at your life, assess how things are at present. Are some aspects of your life more satisfying and rewarding than others? Is there an overall balance in your life or do you spot some aspects which need readjustment? What's missing in your life right now? Is something getting too much attention? Something else too little?

The following Whole Life Review model is designed to help you to assess your current life and your performance in each of your current roles. It gives you a picture which illustrates how you rate your performance in each of your roles as you begin the next year of your life. It also allows you to see clearly the degree to which you feel in balance.

The figure overleaf shows my Whole Life Review, done at the beginning of the year. Notice that each spoke of the wheel represents one of my roles. I rated my performance on each of these roles on a scale of 1 to 10. It gave me the chance to think about my whole life before choosing my Major Focus for this year.

As I was not writing at all at the beginning of the year, Writer was a new role for me. I rated it at 1, my lowest score. I had been investing a great deal of time and energy into my roles as Wife and Coach and the results were satisfying so I rated my performance at 9 on both.

My rating as Homemaker was 7.5 — I was satisfied with the income I was making, and my car, although 8 years old, was still running fine. But I was frustrated because many things that I wanted to do around the home were not getting done. There were overfull files, piles of photos waiting to be put into an album, meals were over-familiar and tired and the plants were drooping or dead... I'm sure you get the picture. Certainly I was not living up to my values as the maker of a home and all that means to me. So overall a 7.5.

My area of greatest concern at this point was my performance in taking care of myself as Jinny's Coach — not a new revelation. I was exhausted and had health problems that I was coping with but not taking care of. While I exercised every day, I wasn't eating well and

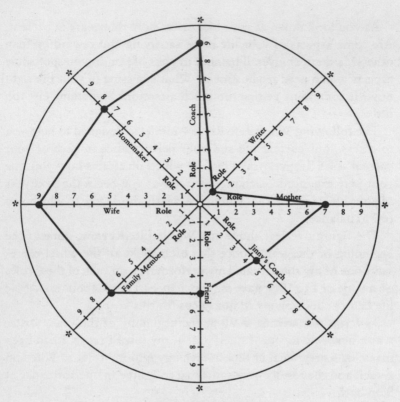

Whole Life Review
Performance and Balance Check

had put on weight and was feeling a bit of a blob. Therefore a 4.5. This highlighted my need to make changes here. It's easy to see by looking at my Whole Life Review where I was out of balance and where I needed and wanted to make improvements.

Before you rate your performance in each of your roles, take a minute to imagine a rating of 10 on each one (be careful of the temptation of thinking you could never earn a 10 on any role!) How would you be acting and behaving if you were achieving a 10 in every role of your life? What results would you see? What would your relationships be like? You are setting your own standards here – so please yourself.

If you have fewer than eight roles, you might want to draw your own circle with the appropriate number of spokes. If you have more, consolidate and integrate your roles until you have eight. Then follow these steps:

USING THE WHOLE LIFE REVIEW:

1. Beside the word **Role** on each spoke, write the name of one of your life roles.
2. Notice that there are ten segments to each line. Use these to rate your performance on a scale of 1 to 10, with 10 – the star at the end of the line – being the highest. For example, if you're completely satisfied with your performance, rate yourself a 10; if you're 50 per cent satisfied, give yourself a 5. If you're not doing anything at all or your performance is abysmal, you'd probably give yourself a 1.
3. Place a dot on each line at the point of your rating.
4. Join the dots as I did to assess your overall level of performance and to gain a visual image of your state of balance.

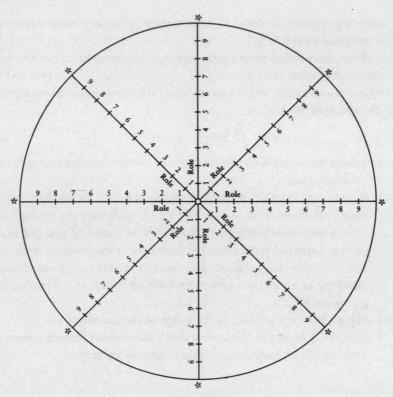

Whole Life Review
Performance and Balance Check

As you look at the results of your Whole Life Review, ask yourself:

- *What do these results mean to me?*
- *What do I see in this overview of my life?*
- *In which role am I performing the worst? the best?*
- *What do I need or want to change first?*

Let your intuition direct your thinking, and listen to your internal messages, both negative and positive. Do your best to make the process validating rather than invalidating. Increase your awareness of yourself as the watcher or the observer – the Chairman of the Board. Use this opportunity to make a neutral assessment of the current reality of your life.

Begin to consider which one of these roles needs your major focus over the next year.

WHY FOCUS?

Life looks less complex and makes more sense when we're engaged in this kind of life review process. As soon as you complete your Best Year Yet workshop, however, the busy-ness of your life will take over once again. In order to stay on the path to the changes you want to make when the day-to-day challenges of living re-emerge, it's vital to select one area of focus that will steer you through your next year. It may sound easy, but life's unexpected interruptions and changes will come as they always do.

SIMPLIFY YOUR LIFE BY INCREASING YOUR ABILITY TO FOCUS.
HARNESS YOUR POWER IN ONE MAIN DIRECTION TO ACHIEVE THE
KIND OF CHANGE YOU WANT TO MAKE.

Think of the Whole Life Review wheel – how do you want it to look in a year's time? Focusing your energies on one role brings a lift in performance – purely as a result of your new awareness.

When you were a child, did you ever do the experiment with the magnifying glass? We were asked to find a dry leaf and let the sunlight pass through the magnifying glass to a spot on the leaf. Before many minutes went by, the leaf caught fire at the exact point where the sun's rays were focused. By directing the energy and power of the sun, something happened and change occurred.

Your personal focus and awareness work in the same way. If you want something to happen, focus on it. Just as the energy and power of the sun fire up the leaf, you can create combustion in your life.

GIVE YOURSELF A CHANCE TO WIN THE GAME YOU'RE CREATING FOR
YOURSELF. WHEN THERE IS ONE ROLE ON WHICH YOU'RE FOCUSED,
YOU FIND NEW LEVELS OF PERSISTENCE AND DETERMINATION.
YOUR TRUE SELF PREVAILS.

As you look at your Whole Life Review, you might ask *Can't I have
more than one focus?* If your chart looks like mine, it looks as if we
must have two or more in order to get back the balance we want.
However, I chose Jinny's Coach as my Major Focus, with an
emphasis on my health. Making myself feel better has, after all, a
positive impact on my performance in all roles. I saw that focusing
on this role would help me to add the new role of Writer to my plate
with a possibility of success. Notice that although Writer had the
lowest score on my wheel, I didn't select it as my Major Focus.
Think carefully, and then choose the focus that will make the most
difference to you.

Having two or more points of focus is a contradiction in terms.
There is no longer a focus and the results can't be the same. One
woman who attended our workshops for many years always had
difficulty choosing. *How can I choose between my role as a Mother
and my role as a Shop Owner? I don't want to give either up and I need
a breakthrough in both. It would be irresponsible to choose one over
the other.* In the end, though, she always found that she had to
choose one; otherwise both suffered. She realized that she could,
without guilt or confusion, choose one that was right for her at that
moment in her life, and that the result would affect all of her roles
for the better.

If you find yourself wanting to focus on two roles, ignore your
inner pleas. There may be a feeling that you want to push hard now
that you've decided to take charge of your life. But trying to do too
much at once will be difficult and might lead you to give up alto-
gether. Then you'd have a bigger problem than having only one
Major Focus – you'd have none.

HOW TO CHOOSE

To help you select your Major Focus, ask yourself these questions:

- *If I could put one problem behind me, once and for all, what would it be?*
- *In which role do I want to have a breakthrough?*
- *If I were able to put a big tick beside one of my roles at the end of the year, signifying that I felt a sense of mastery in that role, which would it be?*
- *What's the biggest impediment to my success and happiness right now?*
- *Which aspect of my life is the biggest drain on my energy and willingness to go for it in life?*

When we think about it, there is often one aspect that's the principal barrier for us. It feels as if there's something in your face and you can't breathe. No room to move. Increase your awareness of the biggest ball and chain you're dragging, weighing you down so you're not able to express yourself fully.

When I thought about these questions in my own Best Year Yet review, focusing on my role as Jinny's Coach and taking care of my health became the obvious choice. I began to imagine racing through my busy life without the pain and exhaustion – moving lightly with great energy – and it was clear to me which role would pay me back the greatest return on the time and energy I invested.

Perhaps, as I did, you'll find your Major Focus by thinking about the different areas of your life rather than the roles you play. These are the role 'subsets' such as money, career, children, health, fitness, long-range planning, love life, marriage, etc. Again, where do you want a breakthrough?

If you do select an area of your life or a quite specific challenge as your Major Focus for this year, it still helps to decide which of your roles would empower you to succeed with this challenge. Choosing a role allows your success to expand past just one area of concern.

In addition to taking much better care of my health, I've already improved my overall performance as my own coach. I find myself listening more to my own good advice and breaking the habit of putting myself at the end of my own TO DO list. Having a role as your Major Focus reminds you to centre yourself in your role and your values as you go for your breakthrough.

Once you've chosen your Major Focus, write it down. Then take a bit of time to envision the success you want to create in this role. What specific and measurable differences do you want to see? What are your criteria for success? What intangible experiences and feelings do you want as a result of achieving this change?

Start to paint a scene in your mind. What would change? What would improve? What would bring a big smile to your face? Create a clear mental picture of exactly what you want.

Think about what you want others to notice and say. Consider the benefits that you want them to experience as a result of your new expertise in living this role.

Before you move on from thinking about your Major Focus, dare to say what you want – and beware of your limiting paradigms. If they cloud your view, remember your new empowering paradigm. Write it down on a piece of paper and below it write your Major Focus. See yourself making a quantum leap in your effectiveness in this role, empowered by this paradigm.

REMEMBER THAT WHAT YOU FOCUS ON IS WHAT YOU GET – FOCUSING YOUR AWARENESS ON THIS ROLE WILL GENERATE THE RESULT YOU WANT.

IT PAYS TO FOCUS

You've now chosen one area of your garden which will get special attention this year. As a result, your entire garden can be much happier and healthier. Focusing on one area raises the standard of the whole.

One of my first clients was starting his own business and found himself in the driving seat for the first time in his career. His investors were pushing him hard to capture major accounts in order to establish the business with a strong base. But he'd never sold a thing in his life and, at this early stage, he couldn't afford to hire a salesperson. So his Major Focus for the year was *Salesperson* – and he hated it!

He recounted stories of forcing himself to pick up the phone and make fifteen contacts a day. He had to push his hand towards the receiver every time, and he'd never been so uncomfortable. But he did it and his focus paid off. By the end of the year, he had a couple of major accounts and overall sales had increased by a factor of ten.

Another older client also focused on his role as *Salesperson* because he wanted to achieve his dream of being one of the top 20 salespeople of the major insurance company he worked with. Every year he struggled and tried, but he never made it to the top. He started by creating a paradigm of success and then visualized his name moving up the list – actually saw his name move to the column in which the top players were listed.

As a result, he began to do all the clever things at once. He realized it was not a lack of knowing what to do that was holding him back. It was a lack of doing it. Success built on success, and when the results were announced at the end of the year, his name was right where he wanted it – on the list of top salespeople.

Another client had a more intangible Major Focus. The role was *Personal Development* and the specific goal was *Crack limiting personal belief systems once and for all!* He attacked the goal with great determination and was able to put his old internal conversations behind him. As a result of his persistence, he was able to stop procrastinating and start taking a stronger leadership role in his company, focusing on his strengths and achievements rather than worrying about other people's opinion of him.

Remember – your Major Focus is not the only thing you'll do this year, just the most important to you.

WHAT ARE MY GOALS FOR EACH ROLE?

'Tis not what man does which exalts him,
But what man would do!

ROBERT BROWNING

THE POWER OF GOALS

People who have goals achieve more results in their lives.

No matter how you define success, achievement is greater among those who have clearly defined goals. It's merely common sense that people who know where they're going have a better chance of getting there. If you don't know your destination, you risk going around in circles, living a life in which you exist but don't really grow and progress.

In my experience the goal factor is the most important distinguishing characteristic of truly effective people. It is far more important, for example, than a person's education or intelligence. Even those who want to meditate on a mountain top have clearly defined goals.

A goal is a specific and measurable result you want to achieve within a specific time frame. It directs you to a destination, a result, a salary, a career, a relationship – something which you haven't yet

---

acquired or experienced in your life.

The results of a study of American business school graduates who had been out of school for at least ten years illustrates the power of goals. Eighty-three percent had no goals, while 14 per cent had vague goals in their minds but no written goals. Only 3 per cent had clearly articulated, written goals. When their level of accomplishment was compared ten years later, those with *some* sense of their goals earned three times more than the ones with no goals, and the 3 per cent with written goals were earning ten times more than those with none at all!

But goals alone are not nearly enough. The setting and achieving of goals may bring a certain brand of success in one narrow aspect of life such as material reward or career promotion, but this does not generate an overall sense of fulfilment. Remember the fallen gods of the 1980s? How many people on their deathbed wish they'd spent more time at the office?

PEOPLE WHOSE GOALS ARE ALIGNED WITH THEIR VALUES ACHIEVE MORE SATISFACTION AND FULFILMENT. WHEN WE'VE ACHIEVED A GOAL WHICH HAS BEEN DRIVEN BY OUR VALUES, BY WHAT WE BELIEVE IN AND WHAT'S REALLY IMPORTANT TO US, WE EXPERIENCE AN UPLIFT IN OUR LIVES AND A SENSE OF FULFILMENT IN OUR HEARTS AND MINDS.

Value-driven goals lead to behaviour and performance which are true expressions of who we are. This in turn leads to the success and satisfaction we've been longing for. The more we repeat this cycle, the more it reinforces our values and our commitment to live in a way that creates a self-perpetuating and self-affirming cycle.

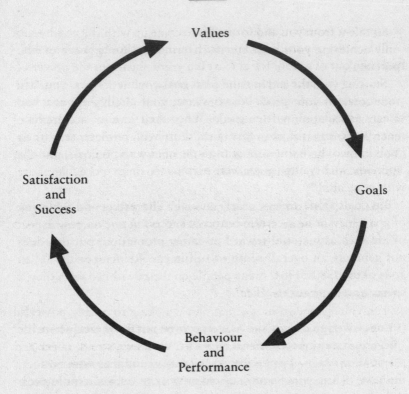

Living within the framework of value-driven goals gives a positive shape to the way you think and feel about your life. You focus on what you want rather than what you don't want, thus providing specific direction and focus for your life. You can move from complaint to action and gain a new degree of momentum – actually moving towards your dreams. A switch takes place and you feel a lift. I can see the sanity return for clients when I ask them, *I understand from what you're saying that you know what you don't want. Now, can you tell me what you do want?*

When you set goals and write them down, you've expressed your willingness to be responsible for living with integrity – doing what you know in order to be true to yourself and your values. Goals pull your talent from you and force you to come up with the goods – not only achieving your goal but discovering and using more of your potential.

Starting with the end in mind pulls both your action and your attitude towards your goals. Your talents, your intelligence and your awareness are pointed at a specific target and your consolidation of energies brings results in a way the scattered approach fails to do. You know whether you're going to Birmingham, Bournemouth or Bologna, and you're on your way.

GOALS GUIDE YOU TO BE RESPONSIBLE AND PROACTIVE IN YOUR LIFE. THE MORE SPECIFIC AND MEASURABLE YOUR GOALS, THE MORE WILLING YOU ARE TO BE RESPONSIBLE FOR MAKING THEM HAPPEN.

POWERFUL GOALS

When you change from wishing and whinging to setting powerful value-driven goals, you move to a more positive and productive life. Negative emotions like frustration, fear, anxiety, stress, anger and depression plague people with no direction and therefore no focus or hope. Setting goals moves us from dreams with a remote possibility and reliance on blind luck to the results and relationships we're looking for. Living life with the attitude, *Let's wait and see how it turns out* is a waste of your potential and your power.

Powerful goals are specific. They are defined in words that give you a clear and concise mental image of what you want to achieve. You know from reading the goal exactly what you want. The more specific your goal the more quickly you'll see what to do and be able to find the resources to achieve it.

Non-specific goal: Spend more time with my children.
Specific goal: Read to my children for at least 30 minutes three times a week.

Non-specific goal: Improve my performance at work.
Specific goal: Find out exactly what I need to do to get a promotion and a 5 per cent pay rise, and do it.

Non-specific goal: Reduce my stress level and increase my peace of mind.
Specific goal: Meditate at least fifteen minutes each morning.

Powerful goals must also be measurable. How many? How big? How often? You quantify each goal so that you'll be in no doubt at the end of the year whether you've won or lost the game or how close you came. If you want a pay rise, how much? So many wealthy people are still working as hard now as when they were 25-year-old hopefuls, and are paying a big price as a result. They've never slowed down to reap the rewards of their success. They don't understand how to cut back since their goal of 'becoming rich' hasn't yet been achieved. They never answered the question *How much?* I've seen many, many examples of this.

Powerful goals must also be set in a time frame. Since you're setting goals for the next year of your life, your commitment exists within a definite amount of time. Limiting the time available to achieve your goal establishes focus. Goals without a deadline are as meaningless as a football match without an agreed ending time.

Once you've set your annual goals, you may want to set deadlines for milestones throughout the year. For example:

Annual Goal: Do a form of aerobic exercise four times a week and lose a stone.
Three-month Milestone: Jog three times a week and lose four pounds.

Annual Goal: Write my first book and find an agent and publisher.
Three-month Milestone: Write chapter outlines and contact three potential agents.

Commitment to a deadline for achieving a goal adds momentum and certainty. You're on your way – a great antidote to procrastination. And the earlier you get started, the more time you have to achieve your goal and therefore the better your chance of success.

Powerful goals start with strong, active verbs. They mark the start of your goal: a simple and complete sentence stating clearly the result you want. Verbs clarify what needs to be done, stimulate a call to action and clearly describe exactly what you want to do. For example:

- Give
- Earn
- Join
- Practise
- Write
- Spend time
- Complete
- Arrange
- Plan
- Get
- Choose
- Invest
- Achieve
- Learn
- Work
- Ensure
- Make
- Meet

Starting your goals with these kinds of words gives you direction and gets the momentum going the minute you write them down.

Finally, learn the distinction between Result Goals and Process Goals – best distinguished by the following examples:

Result Goal: Achieve sales target of £150,000.
Process Goal: Make 20 new sales calls each week.

Result Goal: Lose a stone and a half in weight.
Process Goal: Eat 1200 calories a day with 20 per cent or less calories from fat.

Result Goal: Improve communication and connection with my sons.

Process Goal: Write to my sons every week.

Take time to consider which type of goal is more likely to ensure that your behaviour will be appropriate to achieve the result you actually want. For instance, for years I had weight loss goals – a result goal. Once I switched to a process goal which I knew would guarantee the result, I attained the goal. Process goals define the action we think will lead us to our goal. And, as the point is to make life sweeter on the way to our goals, process goals provide a strong incentive to continue, and rewards along the way. (Remember to celebrate your achievements and congratulate yourself each time you fulfil a process goal!)

However, some goals are far more powerful if they are expressed as result goals. It often takes more courage for me to set this kind of goal, specifically in the area of business, money or fund-raising. Once I learned to make this level of commitment and deliver, however, I was able to take on bigger and bigger challenges and make them happen. Sticking my neck out in this way forced me to dig into myself and come up with the ability to achieve the goal – and, I believe, doing so has pulled out far more of my potential than if I hadn't made such big promises.

SUMMARY OF GUIDELINES FOR POWERFUL GOALS

Goals must:

- Be Specific
- Be Measurable
- Be Time-framed
- Start with a verb
- Appropriate: result or process goal

POWERFUL GOALS ARE SIMPLE, CLEAR INSTRUCTIONS FOR YOU AND YOUR AWARENESS. YOU NOW KNOW WHERE THE BULL'S-EYE IS LOCATED, AND HAVE AN EXCELLENT CHANCE OF HITTING IT.

GOAL-SETTING

It's time to begin to write your goals for your Best Year Yet.

As you switch to Life Pursuit II, you start by setting goals shaped by your personal values. This step alone brings you closer to a life of integrity and satisfaction. While these goals will address your basic wants and needs, they will (more importantly) lead you to a life in which you're true to yourself and therefore fulfilled.

If you have identified your lifetime goals and have a personal vision or mission, some of your goals become self-evident as the year-size step on the way to achieving your longer-term goals. As much as possible, set your goals in the context of your bigger plan.

Tim and I have been working for four years on our 50/57 Plan, which is designed for us to be able to take a sabbatical year when he is 50 and I'm 57. This has focused many of our short-term goals and made it much easier for us to make choices which further this dream. As soon as we first made this plan, we changed our spending habits. We cut back the money we used for eating out, holidays and clothes and increased our mortgage payments. Each year we've set goals for savings, reducing the mortgage and other debts as well as learning more about the places we want to visit and the adventures we hope to have in that year.

Setting Goals in the Context of a Life Plan

Life Goals or Personal Vision → Five-Year Goals → Best Year Yet Goals

Use whatever level of awareness you currently have about your long-term goals. Perhaps this exercise will stimulate you to apply the technology of Best Year Yet to the planning of your life.

As you begin setting your goals, make sure you've thought through which areas of your life are related to each of your roles. For example, the role of *Self Manager* or *Personal Coach* typically includes such areas as health, fitness, education, skill-building, relaxation and fun. There is a space for noting related areas and aspects of each role.

The man whose goals are listed below includes his children, school fees and presents as areas to consider in his role of *Father*. See how he thought through the different aspects of his role and notice how doing this helped him to define his goals for his role of *Father*.

ROLE: *Father*

Areas included: *Joe*   *Julia*   *Presents*
          Mark   *School fees*

Goals:
- *Set up scheme to ensure school fees for Joe.*
- *Plan a special weekend once a month with each child.*
- *Make sure Julia understands her maths.*
- *Pick out a special present for each in early December.*
- *Express praise and appreciation more than correction.*

Begin by selecting one of your roles and writing down all the areas of your life related to it. Then jot down the goals you have for yourself for the next year, remembering the guidelines for setting powerful goals.

Follow your intuition and listen to your inner voice. Rather than being a difficult part of the process, most people find it easy to concentrate quickly as they begin the process of giving specific shape to their next year.

For most of us there's a mental rubbing of hands. Finally, some sanity! You've worked through the first seven steps of the process and you've cleared your mind and made some space for yourself. Your natural enthusiasm is uncovered again and it's time to plant your garden in the rich soil you've prepared.

Remember to set a clear goal for your Major Focus. In Part Three you'll find forms such as the one below for setting goals for each of your roles.

ROLE: _____
Areas included: _____ _____ _____   _____ _____ _____
Goals: ....

ONE FINAL CHECK

One last step before finalizing your goals for your Best Year Yet – a final pass to ensure that you have the best possible chance of achieving your goals. The purpose of this step is to ensure that you are committed to each of your goals, that each has a reasonable chance of success.

Go through your list of goals, thinking carefully about each and asking yourself such questions as:

- *Will I make sure this happens?*
- *Am I merely hoping this will be achieved simply because it's on the list?*
- *Am I going to do this?*
- *Is this goal specific and measurable? Does it start with a verb?*
- *Is it a result or a process goal? Have I made the right choice?*

Make sure that your goals:

1. Match your VALUES
2. Are not 'SHOULD' goals
3. Are ones you WANT badly enough to do what it takes, and
4. Are ones you're willing to be RESPONSIBLE for.

Match your personal values to your goals

Above all, make sure that the goal is aligned with your values. Place your list of personal values beside you as you review your goals. Catch goals which could lead you away from your values. For example, a goal to earn more money might lead you to work longer hours and jeopardize your goal to spend more time with your children. Is it worth it? Is it really necessary?

Remember the cost of goals which are not aligned with your values – can you afford even one year in which you waste energy and intelligence pursuing a goal which violates one of your personal values? If you're in doubt, perhaps the goal is one which chases Life

Pursuit I – proving yourself. If so, give it a toss!

Avoid 'should' goals

Many teachers have reminded me not to *should on myself!*

Are any of your goals ones you feel you should do but don't really want to do? First ask yourself if it's aligned with your principles. If it is and you can see that it's something you really would like to do, shift your attitude to the goal from <u>Should</u> to <u>Want</u> or <u>Will</u>. If you can't do this, cross it off your list.

Sometimes our Shoulds are tired old goals. Let them go. Often we've had goals for decades and never consciously stopped wanting them. When you were seven years old you wanted a fancy bicycle but you never received it. Now that you've grown, it's time to let go of the 'bicycles' in your life.

For example, do you have a dream weight or size which you haven't seen since you were 17? Let it go. Get to a healthy weight and size and drop the impossible fantasy. For years I tried to get to eight and a half stone. Every bite I put into my mouth and every shopping trip was in the context of *Not Eight and a Half Stone!* What a relief it was to finally give up that false goal!

What are the 'bicycles' in your life? Give yourself a break and get them off your list.

Connect to your real wants

The question of whether I really *wanted* to do something was a confusing issue for me until I made a distinction between Little Wants and Big Wants.

Little Wants are really 'don't wants'. The lazy me never wants to crawl out from under the duvet. I want to stay in bed! I mean, who really wants to leap out of bed in the morning? And for sure I never wanted to give up smoking. Give me the easy life. It's so easy to follow this kind of want – sure I'd rather watch television than write letters or ring my mother. I much prefer the extra half hour of sleep to getting out in the cold to exercise.

ENDLESS PROCRASTINATION, DISAPPOINTMENT AND LACK OF
SELF-RESPECT ARE THE PRODUCTS OF THE LITTLE WANTS.

But these Little Wants were not what I *really* wanted. Big Wants are characterized by their connection to my personal values and further my commitment to Life Pursuit II. The achievement of goals in this category are worth the discipline needed for me to make sure they happen. Without this type of goal, I'd rarely grow or make the contribution I'd like to make.

The Big Wants have more integrity than the Little Wants and give you the environment in which you can express yourself.

Responsibility

If you're not willing to do whatever you need to do to achieve the goal, you're probably not going to be responsible for achieving that goal. For each of your goals, you must be motivated to give it your best shot – otherwise, scratch it.

In order to achieve these goals, they'll need focus throughout the year. There are probably plenty of goals on your list – get rid of the ones you're not going to take responsibility for.

WHAT ARE MY TOP TEN GOALS FOR THE NEXT YEAR?

People are always blaming their circumstances for what they are. The people who get on in this world are the people who look for the circumstances they want, and, if they can't find them, make them.

GEORGE BERNARD SHAW

WHY LIMIT MYSELF TO TEN?

When we first started to set goals for the year ahead, Tim and I each had over 100 goals written on our stack of 3 x 5-inch file cards. We had one card for each role, and most had goals written on both sides of the card – a few roles even had several cards stapled together. We failed to limit ourselves by selecting the ones which were most important to us. The goals sat on the list together, each having the same amount of weight, attention and focus. There were simply too many.

While we each did well simply because we'd taken the time to identify roles and set goals for each of them, we robbed ourselves of the satisfaction of creating a game we could win. In doing so we decreased our overall effectiveness and it became too easy to let our attention drift away from our intentions for the year. I gave up on many of mine early in the year because I just didn't have the time for them. I'd set myself an impossible task, but still felt guilty because I couldn't fulfil it. A mistake and a lesson.

While I'm not suggesting that you need to *eliminate* all but ten of the goals you've set, I strongly recommend that you select the ten which are most important to you. You can certainly work on the rest of your goals and achieve them. But selecting your top ten allows you to focus your power in a laser-like way and therefore increase the amount of intelligence and consciousness you can commit to each one. A list of your Top Ten Goals for the next year gives you a map with which to plan your journey. You'll find it easier to attract the support and resources necessary to get to your destination.

When I look at my list of Top Ten Goals and I know I'm satisfied with the goals I've selected, I get that feeling of *Can Do!* I can't wait to get started and I have a strong belief in myself and my ability to stick to the plan and make it happen. It looks possible.

THE QUALITY OF THINKING YOU NEED TO DO IN ORDER TO SELECT YOUR MOST IMPORTANT GOALS FORCES YOU TO MAKE THE CHOICES THAT WILL GUARANTEE BALANCE IN YOUR LIFE AND THE EXPERIENCE OF BEING TRUE TO YOURSELF – THE FEELING THAT YOU'RE GOING TO MAKE TRUE PROGRESS IN THE COMING YEAR OF YOUR LIFE.

HOW TO CHOOSE

Start by reviewing your responses to the first seven questions. Remember what you've learned about yourself and what's most important to you. Think about the lessons you learned and the Guidelines you've established for your next year. Remind yourself of your new paradigm and your personal values.

To start the process of selection, turn back to your Whole Life Review and the thinking that led you to choose your Major Focus. What's going to make the most difference to you in this next year? As you answer these questions and carry out this review, begin to consider prioritizing your goals and choosing the ones that matter most.

MY TOP TEN GOALS FOR NEXT YEAR

1 ....
2 ....
3 ....
4 ....
5 ....
6 ....
7 ....
8 ....
9 ....
10 ....

As you've been taking yourself through the Best Year Yet process, what vision have you started to create for your next year? Think about what you really want for yourself and those people who are most important to you. Consider the benefits inherent in achieving your most important goals – both for yourself and others. Which goals, when achieved, will make the most difference to you and them?

Once you've completed this preliminary thinking, return to the list of goals you set for each of your roles. First highlight or circle the ones which are 'musts' for your list of ten. The obvious ones. Then tally up the number you've selected and figure out how many more you can select to make up your list of ten.

When you have your first draft list of ten, write them down so you can look at them together. Visualize yourself in a year's time having achieved each of these goals. How will you feel then? Will you be thrilled with what you've achieved? Do the goals motivate you to keep going until they're reached? Make sure that you're genuinely enthusiastic about the end you have in mind. Don't sell out. Is it enough, at least for now? If not, find out what's missing and add it.

Next, consider whether it's possible. Can you do it? Look through your list to catch conflicting goals and ask yourself if there's a way you can achieve both goals without sacrificing your values or, perhaps, your health. Dig up any lingering thoughts and doubts and address them. How can you overcome them? Either see how to make it work or switch some of the goals for others you didn't select at first.

Check your list to make sure that each Role has at least one goal, so that your plan leads you to a more balanced life and lifestyle. As you imagine yourself walking and running through the next year of your life, make sure you're happy with the balance of work and play. I recommend that at least one goal on your list be for pure fun or pleasure – at least one you're *really* looking forward to having or doing. This is your life, right?

Finally, make sure that your Top Ten Goals are the design for your Best Year Yet. When you've achieved these goals, will you have had the best year you've ever had? And don't forget, whatever didn't make the cut this year can go on your list next year. The coming year is just your best year so far – they can get better and better as the years go by. Ours truly have.

STARTING TO PLAN YOUR BEST YEAR YET

Once you're happy that you have the right ten, take one last look at the words and the way each goal is written. Revise, rewrite and reword until you're completely satisfied. Keep at it until you're happy that each goal is expressed perfectly and describes accurately the outcome you want.

Write each goal on a separate piece of paper or card and place them in front of you. Look at them together in the context of their being the seeds you're planting in the rich soil of your intelligence and your consciousness. You now have the beginning of a plan for your Best Year Yet. There are a few more steps to take to prepare your plan and make it even more powerful.

The first step is to repeat your new empowering paradigm for the year as you look at each of your goals. Notice how each different goal is empowered by this way of thinking and feeling about yourself.

The second step is to prioritize your list of goals. My favourite definition of **priority** is that which brings me the greatest return on the investment of my time and energy.

Which one will head up your list? Using the definition above, which goal is your top priority for the year? For most people it's the goal related to their Major Focus so that it grabs their attention every time they look at the list. Whichever it is, pick up the card it's written on, turn it over and place it to one side, knowing it will be at the top of your list.

Then look at the remaining nine goals and again ask yourself, *Of the goals left, which one will bring me the greatest return on the investment of my time and energy?*

Let your intuition guide your selection of the goal which will be second on your list. When you've selected it, turn it over and place it on top of the first goal. Repeat this process with all of your other goals until you have a prioritized list of your Top Ten Goals.

The last step is to make a one-page summary of the four principal parts of your Best Year Yet Plan:

1. Guidelines for the Year
   Question Three
2. New Paradigm
   Question Four
3. Major Focus
   Question Seven
4. Top Ten Goals
   Question Nine

Do something to make the page special. Perhaps you'll want to have it typed, or just written neatly in your own hand on a piece of quality paper. Use your imagination to create this important blueprint for your Best Year Yet – it's a very special document.

Now at last you have a one-page summary of your basic plan for the next year. All the work you've done to get to this point has been most important – you've clarified your intention and you know what you want. Even if you simply put your one-page summary in a drawer and then didn't look at it until the end of the year, you would still have a good chance of having your best year yet. Don't underestimate the importance of the thinking you've done in answering the first nine questions.

The figure opposite is an example of one man's Best Year Yet Plan. You haven't met him, but notice how much you know about him and what's important to him from looking at his plan.

Look at your own page, imagining that it's not yours but someone else's. I find this shift in perspective sometimes helps me to appreciate what I've accomplished just by making my plan.

YOUR ONE-PAGE PLAN IS YOUR GUIDE FOR THE NEXT YEAR. IT PROVIDES A FOUNDATION FOR YOUR THINKING AND PLANNING AND GIVES YOU YOUR OWN BEST ADVICE ON HOW TO BEHAVE AND PERFORM IN ORDER TO TURN YOUR PLAN INTO A REALITY.

This plan will form the basis of how you organize and manage yourself to achieve your goals. It helps me to make choices throughout the year and enables me to do a good job of coaching myself on a weekly and daily basis.

Read again your own words of wisdom:

- The good advice you've given yourself with your _Guidelines._
- The empowering _Paradigm_ to guide your perception of yourself.
- Your _Major Focus_ and the breakthrough you're going for.
- Your carefully crafted list of _Top Ten Goals_ for the year.

GUIDELINES FOR MYSELF

- *Be cheery all the time.*
- *Do first things first.*
- *Identify and say what I want.*

New Paradigm

I am a master at creating my own destiny.

Major Focus

Managing Director.

My Top Ten Goals

1 *Practise Gold Time Management every week.*
2 *Meditate daily.*
3 *Achieve our profit target for the year.*
4 *Make a complete plan for my retirement.*
5 *Do all I can to support Sue in her new career.*
6 *Have a special event each month for the kids.*
7 *Exercise five times a week and lose 10lb.*
8 *Host a great reunion for our family.*
9 *Make contact with old friends.*
10 *Ensure all staff receive a monthly coaching session.*

Take a minute to appreciate yourself and the clarity, direction and sense of purpose you've created for yourself. You've now put yourself among that special group who have clearly articulated goals and a plan for their lives. However, you've gone even further. All too often those people who do set goals do so without preparing the personal environment for those goals to succeed. By answering the questions of the Best Year Yet process, you have taken the necessary steps to prepare this environment for yourself.

HOW CAN I MAKE SURE I ACHIEVE MY TOP TEN GOALS?

The problem in my life and other people's lives is not the absence of knowing what to do, but absence of doing it.

PETER DRUCKER

DOING WHAT YOU KNOW TO DO

Ain't it the truth! The quote above summarizes one of the greatest challenges of being human. When I've taken the time to look back at some of my failures – the big ones and the little ones – I can usually see exactly what I could have done differently to reverse my fortune.

The final question of the Best Year Yet process is designed to remind you of what you know to do, and this chapter is devoted to hints and ideas to help you do just that.

One simple key in achieving your Top Ten Goals for the year is *visibility*. Keep your Best Year Yet Plan in sight. Decide where to put it so you'll see it every day. You may want to pin it on the wall near your desk, or clip it inside your diary, inside a cupboard you use frequently or in a prominent place in your filofax. You'll need to decide how public you want to be with your goals – whatever you decide, try to find the solution that ensures *you'll* see them regularly.

Again, awareness is everything. Taking just ten seconds a day to read your plan is one of the best recommendations I can make. Give the page a good chance to grab your attention, stimulate you to thought and action and refocus your intention for the year.

Now that you've made a plan for the year, the following model is invaluable in managing yourself to achieve success. It's a simple reminder of the fundamentals of the Best Year Yet process. The three angles of the triangle (illustrated opposite) point to the key aspects to keep in place to make things happen. I call it **E-S-P**, the foolproof plan – not always easy, but a simple reminder of the basics.

E We often know what to do to achieve our most important goals and meet our biggest challenges. When we're aware of the **External** factors – what we need to do in order to move towards our goal – we're on our way. Take full responsibility for each goal – identify the action needed and take the steps you see to take. Just do it.

S Using a coach, a colleague or a friend – any form of **Support** – helps us identify what we need to do (**E**) and supports us to shift to our empowering paradigm (**P**).

P The way we see the problem, our **Paradigm**, can either lead us to success or failure. Removing internal obstacles makes the greatest difference to our success. Make sure that your focus on your new paradigm is receiving as much attention as your goals. Invest the time to make sure this happens.

E-S-P — The Foolproof Solution

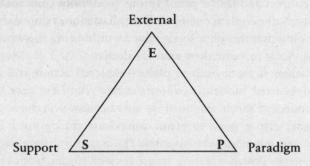

This is the three-legged stool of awareness. Make sure each leg is in place and working and you'll have a simple and stable platform on which to work to deliver your plan. Do what you need to do (E), shift your paradigm to the perception that empowers you (P) and find someone to support (S) you to do the first two.

The balance between (E) and (P) is critical. I've known so many people who seem to be taking all the right action, doing what they know to do but still their dreams elude them. The problem is usually found on the inside, shaped by a limiting paradigm that is arguing against their success the whole time they're busily working on their goals.

THERE MUST BE A BALANCE BETWEEN THE GOAL WE WANT AND
THE WAY WE PERCEIVE OUR CHANCES OF SUCCESS.

Ever met a beautiful person who looks and acts like the kind of person who would be pursued by many potential partners, yet is alone? Most often this is not a matter of choice but a matter of limiting internal messages.

Nor does it work to have a brilliant empowering paradigm and sit waiting for miracles to occur. Sometimes this happens, but taking action which furthers the result on which we've focused our positive paradigm is a guarantee of success. In the 1970s there were many courses and books propagating 'prosperity consciousness'. I saw too many people spending as if they had money they didn't have and hoping that this philosophy alone would bring the wealth they desired. Most just dug themselves in deeper.

But when you put both in place – external action and internal focus – the earth moves. In order to ensure your Best Year Yet, you must not only change what you do but also how you think and feel. Changing either your external behaviour (**E**) *or* your internal mental and emotional environment (**P**) makes a difference but it's not enough. Positive lasting improvement comes from changing both at once. The Best Year Yet process makes sure you do this.

When we're trying to put all this together in the middle of a busy life, it's sometimes difficult to remember these simple truths. The answer lies in the third leg of the stool – support. A few people have mastered the art of self-coaching, but most of us do better if there's a friend or colleague whom we meet on a regular basis to check our progress and see how we're doing. They keep us honest.

Even though we want to move into new territory, we can be so uncomfortable about it we avoid doing what we know to do. Promising someone else that you're going to take action towards your goals or meditate on your paradigm can make all the difference. Years ago when I first wanted to start running I would promise myself day after day that I'd wake up early and get out there – but I rarely made it out the door. What finally made the difference was agreeing to meet a friend at 6:30 a.m. three mornings a week.

If you're wondering where to find someone to support you this year, consider someone else who has completed the Best Year Yet process. You can support one another. Or sometimes couples sit down once a month, review their achievement against their past month's goals and set goals for the next month. You might ask a work colleague – a boss, subordinate, peer – anyone who'd like to be in the kind of relationship in which the partners are committed to one another's success.

SEEK OUT A LIKE-MINDED PERSON IN YOUR LIFE AND PROVIDE SUPPORT FOR ONE ANOTHER. THE SECRET LIES IN YOUR WILLINGNESS TO BE SUPPORTED TO DO WHAT YOU KNOW TO DO.

Use the E-S-P solution to get yourself moving again any time you feel stuck. It's an awareness tool and a catalyst for action. Think about the particular problem or goal and answer these questions to get yourself moving again:

Key Questions

E WHAT'S THE NEXT STEP?
S WHO CAN PROVIDE THE SUPPORT I NEED?
P DOES THE WAY I SEE THE PROBLEM LEAD TO SUCCESS?

PITFALLS

There will be disappointments on the way, but it's possible to avoid many of them by becoming aware of some of the pitfalls and the damage they can do to your enthusiasm. Once you know about them, you can see them coming and side-step them rather than falling into them.

One of the most discouraging influences is the negative and disempowering messages we give ourselves. This kind of internal mental conversation is part of being human. When I hear people talk about some of their fears and doubts – some of the things they hear themselves saying to themselves – I think we must all be tuned in to the same channel. Sounds just like me. It's all part of the social and emotional conditioning that we've received from our environment.

The trick is to catch yourself when you're listening to this station as if it were the God's truth. Change to another station – your new empowering paradigm. The station that dispenses the truth. It's hard to imagine that you'll get the internal voice to shut up. But you can control the attention you give the voice and, above all, where you focus your awareness. One lesson I've heard many times is:

We're not responsible for the thoughts that come into our minds, only for what we do with them.

Another powerful pitfall is the negativity of others. I've seen people so positive and enthusiastic I thought nothing could stop them, yet one discouraging or disparaging remark from someone else and their confidence dissolves. While we can't stop people who *seem* to want us to feel small and stupid, we can ignore them or, better still, stay away from them. Seek out people who support you and want you to succeed. Listen to motivational tapes which remind you of who you are and what you can do. Read books that inspire you to do what you really want to do. Do whatever you can to build up the muscle of your heart and your awareness – your centre, who you are.

Finally, beware of end-goal thinking. It goes something like this: *I don't care what I have to go through this year. I'll make any sacrifice to get what I want!* This approach doesn't lead to your Best Year Yet. Willing yourself to succeed while gritting your teeth is not the name of the game.

CHOOSE YOUR MOUNTAIN NOT FOR ITS SUMMIT, BUT FOR THE CLIMB. ENJOY THE PROCESS.

Things won are done; the joy lies in the doing.

WILLIAM SHAKESPEARE

GOLD TIME

How many times have you been told that what you need to do is manage your time? Good advice, you think, but actually it's impossible. Time is unmanageable. No matter what you do or how well organized you get, the hands of the clock go round and round. What you *can* do, however, is learn to manage *yourself*.

One of the greatest secrets of successful self-management is described by a simple and powerful system I call Gold Time Management. It leads us to manage ourselves by identifying the activities in each of our roles that will make the greatest difference to us and to others.

The following Gold Time model shows how it works.

Gold Time Management

	Urgent	Not Urgent
Important		**Gold Time**
Not Important		

Gold Time is time spent on **Important, not Urgent** activities – or activities in the upper right-hand corner of the matrix. It's called Gold Time because the time you spend on this type of activity pays off at least tenfold over the time you invest in other types of activity.

Also, as the natural movement is for things to move from **Not Urgent** to **Urgent,** by focusing on activities in the upper right-hand corner you're led to a life of less stress and less fire-fighting. Fewer things reach the crisis stage. For example, as a 30-year-old you might feel that it is very important to exercise and get more fit. But it's not really urgent – it can wait.

And it's so easy to wait. You're going to do it but right now you're too busy. We tell ourselves *As soon as I...* (fill in the blank with your reason for postponing what really matters to you). Whatever it is, it comes before you'll devote more time to becoming more fit. As the years go by and the medical check-ups provide more startling feedback, the need might become more urgent. But without awareness of Gold Time, life gets eaten up by the empty promise of '*As soon as...*'

Activities which are **Important, Not Urgent** are activities or projects which matter most to you. For example, your Top Ten Goals for this year. Although you really do want to achieve them and know that you'd feel a lot happier and more fulfilled if you did, your resolve can get eaten up by activities in the other three segments of the model. There's too much that *must* be done (**Important and Urgent**) before you can devote time to your Best Year Yet Plan.

AS GOETHE ONCE SAID, '*THINGS WHICH MATTER MOST MUST NEVER BE AT THE MERCY OF THINGS WHICH MATTER LEAST.*'

The more responsibility you have in your life, the more essential it is to spend time in the upper right-hand corner. For example, business leaders who do not remember this spend much of their time in crisis mode and are never capable of making *lasting* positive change in the culture or the performance of the business.

They realize that it's vital to walk around and get to know the people in the business and listen to them, but their diaries are too full of meetings just now. They know that in order to make any sense of things they must take time out to plan for the future, but first they must prepare the speech for the industry conference next week. They know they should invest in building better relationships with their colleagues on the Board, but right now they have to sort out an emergency. And so life goes on.

The process of changing to this new type of self-management is simple. Do Gold Time activities first! It makes all the difference. Doing so guides us naturally to be true to ourselves and our personal values. This focus creates integrity in the way we lead our lives. Having become better and better at this approach over the years, I have become more sane and have a greater sense of balance. I've come to realize that the only thing I can have power over is myself: when I practise Gold Time self-management, I make full use of that power.

Put your Top Ten Goals first. Put yourself and what you value first. The rest will get done. Promise. Once I've taken a step that brings me closer to one of my Top Ten Goals or helps me to do a better job in one of my life roles, I experience such self-respect and energy that I can attack the urgent activities and get them done in far less time.

My experience has shown that the benefits of Gold Time are:

- Feelings of self-respect, being true to myself.
- Reduction in stress and anxiety.
- Improved performance in all my life roles.
- Fewer last-minute panics.
- Sense of personal power.
- Personal fulfilment.
- End of sacrificing – I'm doing far more of what really matters to me.

THE SYSTEM

Setting up the system to allow you to focus on and achieve your Top Ten Goals is not difficult. It just takes discipline and a focus on what matters most to you. The system is based on common sense which you can easily figure out for yourself – if you want to achieve an annual goal, take little steps regularly throughout the year and you'll get there.

Set Monthly Goals which represent a 30-day chunk of what needs to be done to achieve your Top Ten Goals. Then set Weekly Gold Time Goals which are a seven-day plan to move towards your Monthly Goals.

At the end of each month sit down for 30 minutes and take a good look at your Best Year Yet Plan.

Look at each of your Top Ten Goals and identify the step that needs to be taken over the next month to keep you on the path towards this goal. Then, remembering the guidelines for powerful goals, set a goal which will move you closer to your Best Year Yet. When you've achieved it, you'll see visible progress in your life.

I've found that my monthly list works best if I have no more than ten to fifteen goals. This number allows me to take a step on each of my Top Ten Goals and still be able to include other goals which are currently important to me in living my life roles. Then at the end of the month I review what has happened and figure out what percentage of my goals I've achieved. Rarely 100 per cent, but that doesn't matter. What matters is that I'm aware of how I'm doing and what I need to do next.

At the heart of this system is a Weekly Gold Time Planning session. One week is a time frame that allows us to manage ourselves to do what's most important to us and be true to ourselves. Once you get this system in place, this session takes only fifteen minutes a week.

Once a week – most people select late Friday afternoon, Sunday evening or early Monday morning – sit down with your Monthly Goals and identify steps to take over the next week to further these goals. Some weeks there might be nothing to do. Fine, but at least

Top Ten Goals	June Goals
1 Practise Gold Time Management.	1 Practise Gold Time Management.
2 Prepare fully for trip to India next year.	2 Make a budget for India trip and start savings plan.
3 Take better care of my mother.	3 Ring mother every week.
4 Make annual sales target.	4 Sell £4,000 in new business.
5 Get fit and healthy, reducing body fat to 20% or less.	5 Join a gym and work out three times a week.
6 Make a list of ten books I've been meaning to read and read them.	6 Read Handy's *Age of Unreason*.
7 See friends at least two nights a week.	7 Book to see Sam and Anita and Jay and Sue.
8 Start a journal and keep it up.	8 Buy the journal and write in it at least twice a week.
9 Redecorate the living room.	9 Find the gas log fire I want and buy it.
10 Begin a happy relationship with a woman.	10 Ring Diane and invite her to dinner and film.
	11 Don't drink three nights a week.
	12 Ring my brother and sister.

you know that and you'll know that you're on top of that goal.

Just as important, use this time to consider your roles. In your mind stand in each role, one at a time, and ask yourself *What's the most important thing I want to accomplish in this role this week? What can I do that will make the most difference in this role?* Doing this exercise naturally puts us in touch with our personal values and priorities. Then for each of your roles identify one specific weekly goal based on your answers to these questions.

Your list of weekly Gold Time Goals is a combination of your key goals for each role as well as the steps needed to achieve your Monthly Goals.

THE WEEKLY GOLD TIME PLANNING SESSION IS NOT DRIVEN BY YOUR DIARY NOR BY URGENT TASKS. YOU CAN STILL MAKE DAILY TO DO LISTS TO ACCOMPLISH THOSE KINDS OF THINGS. BUT MANAGE YOURSELF TO ACHIEVE YOUR WEEKLY GOLD TIME GOALS ABOVE ALL.

AGENDA FOR WEEKLY GOLD TIME PLANNING SESSION

1 Review Gold Time Goals for last week and appreciate what you have achieved.
2 Look at Monthly Goals and, when necessary, set weekly Gold Time Goals which move you towards accomplishing each goal.
3 Consider each of your roles, asking yourself the following questions:
  • *What's the most important thing I want to accomplish in this role this week?*
  • *What can I do that will make the most difference in this role?*
4 Set one weekly Gold Time Goal for each role based on your answers.

When I was talking with one client about this system, he had the following reaction: *It's not fair to have just one goal for my role as Managing Director when I have so much more to do in that role than I do in so many of my other roles. Why waste one goal on my role as Father when I've got 18 things to do as MD? Can't I have more than one goal in this role and leave out the others if there's not as much to do about them right now?*

You may be able to appreciate this kind of problem. But it's based on task-thinking and driven by how much there is to do. It is time-based rather than rooted in roles and personal values. The Gold Time system has nothing to do with time. It's designed to make sure that once a week you stop to consider your life and the roles you play in it. It forces you to place yourself in each role for a moment and select one important action to take in each.

Some of your role goals for the week may take only a few minutes, for example, *Ring my mother*. Others such as *Write the first draft of Chapter 3* might take hours. But time is not what the Weekly Gold Time system is about. It's about balance in your life – living your life in such a way that your personal values are not sacrificed in the pursuit of urgent, short-term 'Must Dos'. I came to see that my entire life could be consumed in this pursuit and I'd never ever get to what I really wanted to do. Writing this book is a Gold Time triumph for me. Your answering the Ten Best Year Yet questions is a Gold Time triumph for you.

HAVING SET YOUR GOALS, PUT THEM IN A PLACE WHERE YOU WON'T FORGET THEM AND WILL BE ABLE TO MANAGE YOURSELF TO DO THEM.

My experience is that the principal enemy is our own avoidance of Gold Time activities. Most often we'd rather pick up the phone or make another cup of tea than do what's necessary to achieve the Gold Time goal. The only solution I've ever discovered is summarized by the D word: <u>Discipline</u>.

Discipline is what's necessary – the discipline to stick with it, past the need for a cup of tea, a phone call, a deserved break. Avoid the call of the invisible hand that wants to pull you away from the most important work you want to do; push through the distractions of the mind until the thing is finished. This never seems to get any easier for me but it works every time!

Having put so much thought into developing a clear focus for the week, a little discipline goes a long way.

Makes sense, right? Again, perhaps the most important key to remember in getting yourself to do what you know to do is to set up a support system to make sure you do what you really want to do. When you meet with a coach, friend, colleague or family member once a month to review your goals, you'll find that not only are you more successful in your Monthly Goals but that you'll be plugging into the kind of energy and awareness which empower you to have your Best Year Yet.

PART THREE

THE BEST YEAR YET WORKSHOP

GETTING STARTED

Before you begin your Best Year Yet Workshop, here are a few hints to help you get started on the process and make sure you are as successful as possible.

1. Get in the right frame of mind

I think of this process as 'Time Out!' for myself. I've spent a year in the river of life and now it's time to crawl out on to the bank, have a rest and see how I'm doing.

Tell yourself how much difference this can make to you. A positive mental attitude helps to unblock the hidden barriers to new ways of thinking and behaving.

To inspire myself to make the most of these hours, I do everything possible to make it a stimulating and enjoyable time.

2. Prepare your workspace

Create a special setting for yourself. Clear a desk or table, make sure the lighting is good and make yourself a drink. Do whatever you can to provide yourself with surroundings that are as comfortable and positive as possible. Put on the answer machine or take the phone off the hook. Once you get into the flow, you won't want to be interrupted.

Years ago a friend passed on the hint that Baroque music is an inspiration as well as an aid to creative thinking. It's true. Anytime

I need a boost to get going on a project, I play some Bach or Vivaldi. The effect is magical. Soon after I start listening to this music my mind begins to clear and my ability to concentrate increases. I'm in the flow of what I'm doing and more deeply involved in the project. My natural enthusiasm and motivation increase and I reach that state where I don't want to stop and I don't want to be interrupted. I forget my current frustrations and problems and get into the present moment.

We've used this style of classical music in Best Year Yet workshops – in a room where musical tastes are varied – and the effect has been positive. Bach cantatas, Vivaldi symphonies, Handel oratorios – if you don't have a tape or CD of this kind of music, borrow one – or at least try listening to one of the classical stations and noticing the effect this has on your ability to concentrate and think.

3. Gather your materials

In the following workshop section there are spaces for you to write your answers to the Best Year Yet questions, but any pad of paper will do. You could also make this process an excuse to start a journal, using a notebook or a blank book purchased especially for this purpose. Find your favourite writing pen or pencil and your diary (the latter can serve as a handy reminder of what actually happened over the past year of your life).

Recently I've carried out my annual Best Year Yet on a computer. For those of you who have the equipment and word processing skills, this method provides its own kind of stimulation and has the advantage of being able to print out a copy of your answers as well as the final version of your one-page Best Year Yet plan.

4. Decide whether to do Best Year Yet on your own

You may feel that you want to do this important work on your own, and this certainly works well.

However, many people find that booking a time to do Best Year

Yet with at least one other person makes a difference. They know when they're going to do it – there's a date in the diary – and they feel less likely to back out or procrastinate. It can be good fun as well.

Also, when you do the process with a friend or family member you have a natural partner to meet at regular intervals throughout the year for progress checks and support.

5. A few hints and reminders

While it's possible to do Best Year Yet by staring into space and contemplating the questions, it works better to write your answers down. In this way the process builds on itself and you're able to do a better job. Awareness and consciousness grow, thoughts and perceptions become clearer and important connections are made as you think and contemplate in new ways.

I find myself thinking, '*Oh, yes. I hadn't thought about that before now...*' Having a written record also lets you revisit your notes, flipping pages around and adding to them in an ongoing process of stimulation and realization.

Sitting down and picking up the pen is the hardest part, but I promise you that after ten to twenty minutes you'll catch the wave and be on your way. Trust me.

Allow space for one question per page, or make *this* book your journal and write your answers in the spaces provided. If you're using your own paper, write the question at the top of the page. In any case, start by asking yourself the question and then listening to the response of your heart and mind. Write down whatever comes to you. Avoid the trap of editing and judging. Let your answers flow freely. You can change or add to them later, but to get going just let yourself go.

With each question you'll come to a point where you dry up – there's nothing more at the moment. It's time to move on. You may think of additional answers later, so leave room for them.

Whether you're alone or with others, Best Year Yet is a private and personal exercise and you may find that you want to keep it that way. However, at the end there will be four answers which will form your Best Year Yet Plan, including your goals for the year; you may want to share these with others in order to tap into their support and encouragement.

USE THE PROCESS OF ANSWERING THESE QUESTIONS TO REACH WITHIN YOURSELF AND ANSWER THE QUESTIONS AS HONESTLY AS YOU POSSIBLY CAN. TELL THE TRUTH TO YOURSELF, ABOVE ALL. NO ONE ELSE NEED EVER SEE WHAT YOU'VE WRITTEN BUT IT'S IMPORTANT THAT YOU DO.

PURPOSE

The first item on the agenda for the workshop is clarifying the Purpose and Aims of the workshop. Year after year it's been com-

---

THE PURPOSE OF THE WORKSHOP IS TO MAKE NEXT YEAR YOUR BEST YEAR YET

Aims of the Workshop:

1 *Acknowledge and appreciate what happened last year.*

2 *Define useful lessons.*

3 *Create a positive internal focus for producing results.*

4 *Identify your Top Ten Goals.*

5 *Learn a system of planning to ensure success.*

---

municated in the workshop in much the same way.

THE BEST YEAR YET QUESTIONS

1. WHAT DID I ACCOMPLISH?

Remembering the hints at the beginning of this chapter, begin to write your responses in the spaces below. To answer the first two questions, think back over the past year and write down your responses as you ask yourself each question.

....

....

....

....

....

....

....

....

....

....

....

....

....

....

....

....

2. WHAT WERE MY BIGGEST DISAPPOINTMENTS?

3. WHAT DID I LEARN?

As you reflect back over the past year, think about what you've learned. These can be life lessons you've actually learned and put into practice or lessons you could learn, given what happened. Just ask yourself the question and write your answers as they occur to you. Don't let a thought go by – put it down.

In order to remember all your lessons and potential lessons, look back at your list of accomplishments and disappointments. As you write your responses, state them in the form of clear, straight advice. Write your answers as an instruction. Leave no doubt about what you're to do if you're to follow this lesson. Keep going until you feel you've mined all the gold available from your experience of the past year.

Which three lessons above would make the most difference to you if you followed them in the next year of your life?

Select your top three lessons and write them below. These are your Personal Guidelines for next year. Start each with a verb and make them as short and memorable as possible.

GUIDELINES FOR NEXT YEAR

1. ....

2. ....

3. ....

---

4. How do I limit myself and how can I stop?

In order to have your Best Year Yet, make sure the way you're thinking about yourself and your goals empowers you to succeed. A transformation occurs when you place yourself at the centre of your life, creating your world rather than letting circumstances dictate your success. You can use your intelligence and your power to create a new reality for yourself.

The most powerful tool for personal transformation is the paradigm shift. A paradigm is a way of seeing and thinking about yourself, someone else, an aspect of your life – anything. Some of our paradigms do empower us, e.g., *I've always been good at maths*. However, some are limiting paradigms, such as *I'm not the kind of person to make much money*.

These next questions are designed to help you discover how you're limiting yourself by having assumptions about yourself that lead to failure rather than success. Start by answering the questions below:

How do I limit myself?

In which areas of my life am I not achieving what I want?

....
....
....
....
....
....
....
....
....
....

What do I say about myself to explain these failures?

....
....
....
....
....
....
....
....
....
....

Your answers to this last question are your limiting paradigms. With these perceptions and points of view, what results do you achieve? Where do they lead you? We feed these notions with our intelligence and awareness and then get results which are consistent with them. Life is a self-fulfilling prophecy.

Look at your list and mark the paradigm which has the *strongest* negative influence on you at this point in your life. Which one do you really buy into? Select this one to shift to a new empowering paradigm for your Best Year Yet.

Write a new paradigm that knocks this limiting perception on the head. Make sure that it meets the following criteria for an empowering paradigm:

- Positive
- Personal
- Present tense
- Powerfully stated
- Pointing to an exciting new possibility

Here are several examples:

- I empower myself to have what I want.
- I have the talent I need to succeed.
- In this moment I'm creating a great new future for myself.
- I'm able to go beyond my limitations.
- I've never been so healthy and alive.
- Whatever I put my mind to, I achieve.

NEW PARADIGM

_____

_____

_____

---

5. WHAT ARE MY PERSONAL VALUES?

Think about what's most important to you in your life. What are the hidden drivers behind your more tangible goals? What values do you want to demonstrate in your life?

Our personal values provide the strongest motivation for change and for achieving the goals we most want to achieve. Personal values are stated in one or two simple words which represent the principles that are most central to our lives and who we are.

Examples are values such as integrity, honesty, compassion for others, keeping promises, taking care of myself, loving and so on. Turn to pages 110–111 for further ideas.

To remind yourself of this foundation as you start to plan your next year, list your personal values.

6. WHAT ROLES DO I PLAY IN MY LIFE?

Looking at your life from the perspective of the roles you play provides an invaluable way of integrating the various areas of your life while placing yourself and your personal values at the centre. Your roles provide the framework for goal-setting and planning for your next year; examining them is the best way to ensure that you create balance in your life.

Write a full list of all the roles you're currently playing, such as mother, wife, daughter, friend, manager, homemaker, etc. See the list on page 119 for other possibilities. You can add any new role you'd like to take on in the next year of your life – sailor, writer, poet, actor, student. Do you have a new dream role for next year?

....

....

....

....

....

....

....

....

....

....

....

....

Consolidate your list of roles so that you have no more than eight – fewer is fine. Integrate several roles under one title, if necessary. The purpose of consolidating is to ensure that you are able to give each role sufficient attention.

1 ....
2 ....
3 ....
4 ....
5 ....
6 ....
7 ....
8 ....

7. WHICH ROLE IS MY MAJOR FOCUS FOR NEXT YEAR?

Think about your personal values and how you want them to influence and direct the way you play each role. Look at the Whole Life Review below and use it to assess your **current** performance in each of your roles.

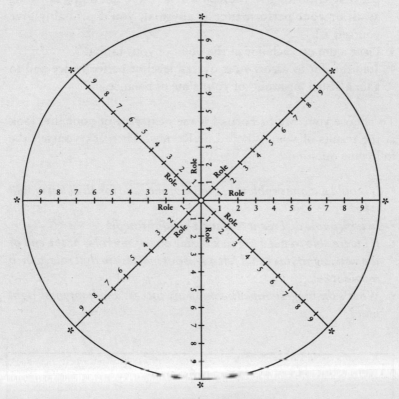

Whole Life Review
Performance and Balance Check

HOW TO USE THE WHOLE LIFE REVIEW

1. Beside the word **Role** on each spoke write the name of one of your life roles.
2. Notice that there are ten segments to each line. Use these to rate your performance on a scale of 1–10, with 10 – the star at the end of the line – being the highest. For example, if you're completely satisfied with your performance, rate yourself a 10; if you're 50 per cent satisfied, give yourself a 5. If you're not doing anything at all or your performance is abysmal, you'd probably give yourself a 1.
3. Place a dot on each line at the point of your rating.
4. Join the dot to assess your overall level of performance and to gain a visual 'printout' of your state of balance.

To choose your Major Focus for the next year of your life, look at the results of your Whole Life Review. Then ask yourself the following questions:

- *If I could put one problem behind me, once and for all, what would it be?*
- *In which role do I want to have a breakthrough?*
- *If I were able to put a big tick beside one of my roles at the end of the year, signifying that I felt a sense of mastery in that role, which would it be?*
- *What's the biggest impediment to my success and happiness right now?*

MAJOR FOCUS

_____

---

8 . WHAT ARE MY GOALS FOR EACH ROLE?

Before you begin to think about the specific goals you have for the next year, take the time to decide which areas of your life are connected with each of your roles. For example, the role of Homemaker could include cooking, decorating, paying bills, and so on.

There follows a form for each of your eight roles; write the name of a role on each form. Fill in the areas of your life in the designated section for each.

Set goals for each of your roles, keeping in mind that powerful goals must:

- Be specific
- Be measurable
- Have a deadline
- Start with a verb

You may want to check the section on this question in Part Two (pages 139–143) for further information about setting powerful goals.

Once you've written your goals, check each goal to make sure that it is aligned with your personal values and that you're willing to do whatever it takes to achieve each one. If not, cross the goal off the list!

ROLE: _____

Areas included: _____ _____ _____
_____ _____ _____

Goals:

....
....
....
....
....
....
....

ROLE: _____

Areas included: _____ _____ _____
_____ _____ _____

Goals:

....
....
....
....
....
....
....

ROLE: _____

Areas included: _____ _____ _____

Goals:

....
....
....
....
....
....
....

ROLE: _____

Areas included: _____ _____ _____

Goals:

....
....
....
....
....
....
....

ROLE: _____

Areas included: _____ _____ _____
_____ _____ _____

Goals:

....
....
....
....
....
....
....

ROLE: _____

Areas included: _____ _____ _____
_____ _____ _____

Goals:

....
....
....
....
....
....
....

ROLE: _____

Areas included: _____ _____ _____
                    _____ _____ _____

Goals:

....

....

....

....

....

....

....

ROLE: _____

Areas included: _____ _____ _____
                    _____ _____ _____

Goals:

....

....

....

....

....

....

....

9. WHAT ARE MY TOP TEN GOALS FOR NEXT YEAR?

Before you select your ten most important goals, review your responses to the first seven questions to remind yourself of what really matters to you and why.

Review all the goals you've set for each of your roles and select the ten which mean the most to you and which will, when achieved, make the most difference to you. Once you have made your choices, check the list again to make sure you're happy with the balance of roles and values. Anything left out? Anything getting too much or too little attention?

Prioritize your list, putting your Major Focus first and the rest in descending order of priority.

TOP TEN GOALS
1 ....
2 ....
3 ....
4 ....
5 ....
6 ....
7 ....
8 ....
9 ....
10 ....

Rewrite the basics of your Best Year Yet Plan in the spaces below.

BEST YEAR YET PLAN

Guidelines

1 ....
2 ....
3 ....

New Paradigm

....

....

....

Major Focus

....

My Top Ten Goals

1 ....
2 ....
3 ....
4 ....
5 ....
6 ....
7 ....
8 ....
9 ....
10 ....

10. HOW CAN I MAKE SURE I ACHIEVE MY TOP TEN GOALS?

You know what to do to achieve your goals. Write your responses to this question – your best source of advice in making this your Best Year Yet.

....
....
....
....
....
....
....
....
....

The secret is to set up a system to ensure that you do what you know to do. Sanity and success are the result of doing the important things first.

Read about Question Ten in Part Two (beginning on page 157) and learn to use The Gold Time System to win the game:

1 Set Monthly Goals to progress your Top Ten Goals.
2 Set Weekly Goals to progress Monthly Goals.
3 Focus on roles and personal values rather than tasks.

Finally, empower yourself to win the game by surrounding yourself with positive friends and colleagues and supportive materials – anything which keeps you in touch with yourself and what matters most to you.

BEST YEAR YET PLANS

You might find it helpful to read several plans written by others to get a sense of how they have approached this most personal process. These people are from different circumstances and range in age from 24 to 49.

BEST YEAR YET PLAN

Guidelines

Be in charge of my money.

Trust and respect my wife.

Be nicer to others.

New Paradigm

I'm a great person and liked by others.

Major Focus

Financial Manager.

Top Ten Goals

1. *Make no unnecessary purchases for the first six months.*
2. *Do my share of work in the house and the relationship.*
3. *Work out four to five times a week.*
4. *Fix mistakes in our credit rating.*
5. *Listen to others and treat them as equals.*
6. *Gain respect above and below me as an officer.*
7. *Build up £1000 in savings.*
8. *Start automatic withdrawals from salary for investment.*
9. *Lose my belly.*
10. *Trust my wife.*

BEST YEAR YET PLAN

Guidelines

Set aside time for myself and my husband.

Enjoy the good in life.

Be aware of all aspects of communication.

New Paradigm

I have the ability and mindset to take the opportunity to excel in all aspects of my life.

Major Focus

Career Woman.

Top Ten Goals

1. *Take control of all aspects of my life.*
2. *Improve my weight and self-confidence.*
3. *Concentrate on all areas of my relationship with my husband.*
4. *Take time out for myself.*
5. *Appreciate what I do have, not what I don't.*
6. *Manage credit and finances.*
7. *Be successful without sacrificing myself.*
8. *Don't forget about my friends and family — make time for both.*
9. *Live for today, not for where I wish I was today.*
10. *Protect myself more by not giving all of me away.*

BEST YEAR YET PLAN

Guidelines

Surrender.

Trust.

Keep opening my heart.

New Paradigm

My magnificence is obvious.

Major Focus

Building a new life.

Top Ten Goals

1. Establish myself as a herbalist and work in a clinic.
2. Create the financial condition to be ready to move.
3. Do one spiritual retreat.
4. Spend some time with my mother.
5. Attract a loving partner who fits and empowers me.
6. Be strong and healthy and keep my weight between nine stone and nine stone five.
7. Deepen my commitment to spiritual practice.
8. Have this year flow magically for me.
9. Increase my knowledge of herbs and Tibetan medicine.
10. Give up smoking once and for all.

THE CREATORS OF THE WORKSHOP

The Best Year Yet workshop would have been a one-off wonder were it not for the hundreds of people who have participated in the process over the years, who have shared their thoughts, ideas and experience. They are the source of this book and the wealth now available. Here are a few of their stories. (I've given them new names to protect their anonymity.)

Paul, a **40-year-old General Manager** with years of experience in large multinational organizations, is now in his second year of planning his life in this way. More than anything he appreciates the ongoing need to fence off Gold Time. *I'm much better at it, but it's a hard slog.* He says most of his success so far is a result of a newfound ability to tell people he's booked or busy when there's no appointment in his diary – only time to do the most important activities.

> I think there are about four phases in this process. First there's the novelty of the idea; then the guilt sets in along with quite a bit of struggle to do what really matters. Finally the change really starts to happen and it feels like a rebirth. I'm looking forward to the final phase when it's all automatic – like brushing my teeth!

Hannah, a **48-year-old mother, grandmother and acupuncturist** is also in her second year of this process. She appreciates tackling one main area of her life so it becomes the predominant theme in her life for the year. *Things happen over the year which are connected to this focus – many things happen, especially letting go of stuff I don't need.* She's learned to be far more flexible in the process and far less guilty when something doesn't turn out as she hoped. Because everything doesn't happen just the way she planned it doesn't mean there's anything wrong with her.

Seeing that I'm not living the way I want to be has been difficult. I have to admit that I've been postponing a lot of things that are dear to me. Now's the time.

Joseph, one of the earliest participants in the workshop who started by taking the course and was soon leading it himself, is a 32-year-old MD of a successful international consulting firm. As a participant in the process since 1981, he talks about *having a much, much higher level of confidence that I can do what I need to do. The most important secret has been getting help when I needed it. I know that a large part of what holds me back is something I can do something about. But the most difficult part is not getting back into the old groove – it's hard to keep this level of awareness over a long period of time.*

Another long-time player is Anne, a 51-year-old successful actress and writer. Overall she feels her biggest win is that she's learned to make progress on the things that matter – for example, although meditation was an attractive notion for many years, it's now moved to being the focal point of her life.

I'm getting more and more honest with myself about setting goals. When things are not working, I can now tackle it. But it's a gentle process of being more honest about my performance overall. After all this time, I see that the quality of my life is far more important than success and achievement in one area of my life.

Peter, a 40-year-old co-founder of a leading financial services marketing group, feels that sticking with this process for over ten years has given him a strong competitive advantage. It's so important, he says, to get away from the process of day-to-day phone calls and TO DO lists and do the important things – otherwise they just drift.

Most difficult for him is trying to do it on his own. Every time he's tried it this way, he's not done so well. *The combination of peer pres-*

sure and peer support makes a difference – even though the people I get together with have no real bearing on the goals themselves. It doesn't matter. He too cites a shift from a life that's work-orientated to a focus on the quality of his life.

Finally the experience of Michael, who describes himself as a **49-year-old successful actor who's learning the hard way.** This experience has helped him sort out a major difficulty dealing with the *stuff of life.* For years he avoided really tackling either the problems in his life or his dreams – feeling a combination of unworthiness and disinterest. Now that he's learned to deal with this aspect of his life, there's more room for his inner self – the part that really matters to him.

> There's a new inner voice speaking to me. When good things happen, it says 'It's OK, you deserve this' – rather than the old inner voices which warned me that it wouldn't last. The most difficult part now is that I get over-confident and lapse into a bit of a daze and then fall into a hole. Constant awareness is necessary and I'm not there yet.

There are so many stories to tell of friends, clients and family who have started to match the promise of their potential. From day one my strongest motivation has been for people to see their gifts as clearly as they are seen by the rest of us – and to honour themselves by having their dreams come true. The world is a better place every time this happens.

Most people have all the talent, skill, awareness and ambition they need, but it's often hidden under a cloud of self-doubt, past disappointments or by simply being too busy. We rarely take time to examine what we're doing or why we're doing it. The material in this book is designed for life planning – by creating a greater consciousness and awareness of the goals, targets and objectives that are in line with what you want for yourself in all aspects of your life, I hope you will be happier, healthier and truly more successful in all you do.

FURTHER READING

Buzan, Tony, *The Mind Map Book*, BBC

Carnegie, Dale, *How to Stop Worrying and Start Living*, Reed Consumer Books

Chopra, Deepak, *Ageless Body, Timeless Mind*, Rider

Covey, Stephen R., *The Seven Habits of Highly Effective People*, Simon & Schuster

Givens, Charles J., *Super Self*, Simon & Schuster

Handy, Charles, *The Age of Unreason*, Random House Business Books

Hay, Louise, *You Can Heal Your Life*, Hay House

Lencioni, Patrick, *Five Dysfunctions of a Team*, Jossey-Bass

Redfield, James, *The Celestine Prophecy*, Warner Books

Rinpoche, Sogyal, *The Tibetan Book of Living and Dying*, HarperCollins

Siegel, Bernie S., MD, *Prescriptions for Living*, Harper Perennial

FIND OUT MORE ABOUT BEST YEAR YET

It's now been 25 years since we developed the Best Year Yet system, and we're proud to say that the results have been extraordinary.

If you're interested in finding out more about Best Year Yet, how to have a best year yet, year after year, in your life and your business, visit www.bestyearyet.com to make your plan online, find a coach and learn much more about how to produce the results you want and need in every aspect of your life.

We now provide programmes for individuals, couples, families and people who work together. Because of the demand that's been created for our programmes, we're looking for people who want to join our global community of Best Year Yet coaches and programme leaders. If you enjoy this kind of work, click on the Careers section of our website.

We also work with organizations to enable business leaders and executives to close the gap between their strategic plans and their performance. We now operate in 14 countries – contact us through our website to investigate having this kind of result in your business.

To find out more about Best Year Yet in the UK and Ireland, contact Area Director Ralph Peters on 01420 89568